W9-BXY-443

ACCLAIM FOR

Everyday Parents Raising Great *Kids*

"There are a lot of parenting books out there, but Dr. MacArthur's is unique. He emphasizes how to have an 'intentional family,' which is increasingly difficult in today's complex society, and he focuses on parenting processes that lead to successful outcomes for children and parents. His book is more than just principles; it promotes action by parents. The self-assessments and guidelines for improving your parenting are solid and will be effective in creating positive changes in your family."

—DR. JEFFRY H. LARSON
CERTIFIED FAMILY LIFE EDUCATOR,
ASSOCIATE EDITOR OF *FAMILY RELATIONS JOURNAL*,
AUTHOR OF *THE GREAT MARRIAGE TUNE-UP BOOK*

"Dr. MacArthur helps parents understand themselves as well as their family of origin. In addition to offering insights related to past family experiences, the author highlights reasons that parents may parent the way they do, and he offers lasting advice and ideas to better meet the needs of current family members. Especially valuable are the many opportunities to examine and then rate one's own level of performance on certain parenting or home environment issues. The ideas to improve and enrich family life are simple yet powerful . . . and give the book the hands-on feel that many parenting books lack. I would recommend this book not only to parents but also to grandparents and anyone who has influence in the lives of children."

—DR. RICK MOODY
CLINICAL PSYCHOLOGIST, AND

—CAROL MOODY
SPEECH LANGUAGE PATHOLOGIST

"Dr. MacArthur has a positive approach that does not pull any punches for parent or child. His book is an easy and thought-provoking read. I encourage both parents and others to read it to discover the essence of their existing family or their family of origin."

—THOMAS J. KENNEDY III, M.D.

"This book is a wonderful resource for any parent who wants to learn the secrets to raising healthy, happy, well-adjusted children. Dr. MacArthur offers heartfelt guidance based on years of experience filled with love and laughter. This book challenges me as a parent to take an active role in shaping my children's self-esteem and identity. What stands out about this book is that anyone can be successful as a parent . . . as long as he or she is willing to lead, love, and commit fully to each child. I love the Blackboard Concept in the chapter on 'intentional parenting.' I believe Dr. MacArthur's book holds the answers to the questions all parents have about how to have a happy family."

—KRISTY M. FORARE
CLINICAL PSYCHOLOGIST

"I have seen Dr. MacArthur's work help countless people overcome their challenges and go on to lead successful lives and raise successful families. Now his expertise and experience are available to everyone. *Everyday Parents Raising* Great *Kids* is powerful and empowering! If every parent in the world would read this book and apply its principles, the majority of the world's problems would be solved."

—ANITA STANSFIELD
AUTHOR OF *REFLECTIONS*

"Reading this book is like having a discussion with a wise father figure. It makes explicit the need to consciously attend to the important duties of being a parent and not to sleepwalk through the process. *Everyday Parents Raising* Great *Kids* should help family interactions become more conscious and purposeful."

—DRS. MIKE AND JENNY BROOKS
CLINICAL PSYCHOLOGISTS

Everyday Parents
Raising *Great* Kids

Everyday Parents Raising *Great* Kids

JAMES D. MACARTHUR, PH.D.

SHADOW
MOUNTAIN

© 2004 James D. MacArthur

All rights reserved. No part of this book may be reproduced in any form or by any means without permission in writing from the publisher, Shadow Mountain®. The views expressed herein are the responsibility of the author and do not necessarily represent the position of Shadow Mountain.

Visit us at shadowmountain.com

Library of Congress Cataloging-in-Publication Data

MacArthur, James D.
    Everyday parents raising great kids / James D. MacArthur.
      p.   cm.
    Includes index.
    ISBN 1-59038-305-2 (pbk.)
    1. Parenting. 2. Family—Psychological aspects. I. Title.
HQ755.8.M314 2004
649'.1—dc22

                         2004008686

Printed in the United States of America   18961
R. R. Donnelley and Sons, Crawfordsville, IN

10 9 8 7 6 5 4 3 2 1

To the memory of
Lorraine Stella Cooper MacArthur
my mother

Contents

Acknowledgments

In the writing and preparation of the manuscript for this book, I am indebted to a number of people. I would have given up many times if not for the encouragement of my wonderful and loving wife, Sherri, who just would not let me quit. She made many sacrifices to help me find the time to write the book. My oldest son, Toran, spent numerous hours reading and editing the manuscript. Susan Easton Black and Anita Stansfield kept me going and gave me much encouragement. Maria Ilieva, a student editor, helped greatly in making my writing more readable. My editor at Shadow Mountain, Janna DeVore, gave me much needed advice, and product director Chris Schoebinger kept the project alive. I also acknowledge many others who read the manuscript and gave me feedback about its potential to benefit families.

On a much more personal note, I have been a father for thirty-five years. I have ten children, ages twenty-two to thirty-five. I have been a grandfather for seven years. I have sixteen grandchildren, ages a few months to seven years.

I have learned a lot from the parenting and grandparenting I have done. Likewise, I have learned a great deal from my twenty-five years as a psychologist. This book is based on what I have gained from all those family experiences. As I share it with you, I hope it comes across as encouraging and enlightening.

I would like to acknowledge all those in my family whom I love and who have been so good to me. I hope we are always together. I am going to name each one individually because that is in keeping with what I write about in this book—the importance of each person in the family.

First comes my companion and the mother of our ten children. I married Sherri McUne MacArthur on June 1, 1968. She is an amazing person. What she has offered to her children over the years is impossible to put into words. Together we are the parents of Toran, David, Paul, Mike, Lindi, Lori, Don, Debbie, Mark, and Sharolyn, and the grandparents of (in order of birth) Michael Niu, Tori MacArthur, Alexis MacArthur, Ben Niu, Emma MacArthur, Noah MacArthur, Allyson MacArthur, Cooper MacArthur, Brayden MacArthur, Isaac Niu, Jacob MacArthur, Sam MacArthur, Avery Niu, Reagan MacArthur, Parker Shumaker, and Reese MacArthur.

Being a father and a grandfather to my loved ones is by far the most important thing in my life. Being a father-in-law to Christopher Niu, Erin Leavitt MacArthur, Monica Nelson MacArthur, Melissa Robles MacArthur, Jennifer Carter MacArthur, Jme Meier MacArthur, and Rodger Shumaker is just frosting on the cake. The accomplishments and honors of my life are important to me, but they pale in comparison to being a part of this family. Were it not for my family, I would never have written this book. I wrote it initially for them. I dedicate it to them.

Prologue

Not all books have a prologue, but this one does. It does because I wanted to tell you why I wrote this book and why I think I have something to say.

First, I would like to establish my commitment to the family. I am writing about the family in a firm spirit of devotion to it. I believe that when two people join their lives together they make a moral commitment to each other and to any children born to them. They commit to live life together as well as they can and to provide their children with a healthy and functional environment in which they can grow to adulthood.

The world is very complex. People often feel alone and overwhelmed. They seek a place where they can talk, play, help each other, learn together, work toward commonly held life objectives, and love and care about each other. They want a place that provides support they can count on. I call that place *the family*. This book is about that place.

This is not a professional book written from the perspective of research. I have read a lot about the family, thought a lot about the family, and decided to write this book from *a personal perspective*. If you read it thoughtfully and find places where you feel like saying, "I disagree," I will be happy. That means you are a thoughtful reader and have reacted to something important. This book is not written from the point of view of "being right." It is a heartfelt representation of the things I have learned in raising my own family and working professionally with many individuals and families. I am not sure I can adequately express how much I want to help people with their families. There is no personal investment we can make that is more significant than what we choose to put into our families. *Families are where the most important things happen.*

While growing up, I saw what appeared to be some very good and healthy families. I also saw families who struggled. I became intrigued with what constitutes a healthy family when I married Sherri McUne of Burns, Oregon. We began a family that ultimately included ten children born in a period of twelve years. Sherri and I had four little boys and then two consecutive sets of twins less than two years apart. At that point in the evolution of our family we had eight children, the oldest being seven. At the time of the birth of our ninth child, our oldest was nine. After the birth of our last child, we had ten children, and our oldest was twelve. That rather large family has taught us a lot over the years. Some of the lessons we learned about family life are in this book.

What constitutes a healthy and happy family? Sherri and I were not sure we knew initially. We have a large and complex family, a natural laboratory in which we are continually learning about family life. We are still trying things out, hoping we can learn and get better at it. The whole experience challenges us to the max. We have worked hard at it and tried to learn from our experience and mistakes. We have also learned from the experiences of other parents we know who are trying to raise their children. Parenting in our own family has been a wonderful experience at times and, at other times, frustrating and highly overwhelming. Most parents would probably agree.

My professional work has also focused on the question of what makes a healthy family. Three months after our second set of twins was born, I completed my Ph.D. in counseling psychology. Two years later I became licensed as a psychologist in the state of Utah. Many years have elapsed since then. I have spent thousands of hours with individuals, couples, and families, helping them with their family struggles, hopes, and dreams. My counseling practice has taught me a lot. I keep asking myself, "What is it that families ought to pay attention to?" That has been the quest of my professional life for many years. I have taught young adult development at the university level for thirty years, and I ran a residential treatment program for troubled youth. I conducted psychoeducational group sessions at the Utah State Prison and learned much from the inmates' stories of their upbringing.

I have always wanted to help families be happy, healthy, and strong. This is my contribution to your family as well as my own. I believe in what I have written, and a copy of this book is going to each of my ten children, who all managed to survive growing up at my house. I love each of them very much. I have worked hard to make these writings sensible and meaningful for their benefit, as well as yours. It is a product of my personal, family, and professional experiences, and it is sincerely and lovingly written.

I now pass it on to you, the reader, hoping it will give you inspiration and practical ideas you can use the minute you begin reading it. I hope as you finish this book that you will feel encouraged and inspired about your family. I hope it will help you understand the key fibers that make up the family tapestry so that you can wrap your loved ones in the warmth and strength of a healthy family.

Finally, I believe that regular, everyday parents like you and me have a big job to do as we attempt to raise our families. I hope you'll join with me, a regular parent, in trying to learn some things about how to do this big and important job.

CHAPTER I

The Family–A Major Commitment

I have always wanted to write a book about families. And I have often wondered why I had such strong feelings about it. Was it because I wanted the United States to be a better place? Or France to be a better place? Or Nigeria? Or Mexico or Japan to be better places?

I do hope for a more stable world in general, but my emotion about strengthening families was greater than just wanting the world to be a better place. What was it I really wanted? Finally it hit me. I wanted *my* children and grandchildren to be in a happier and healthier place! I was thinking of myself! I wanted each one of them to be in a setting where they would feel important, valuable, worthwhile, significant, and competent. I had a deep, deep desire to create an environment where the people I loved could experience those things, be happier, and enjoy greater well-being. There are strong influences in the world today that would like to bring our children down. I want to fight against those influences. I believe the family is the first line of best defense. So, where is that place, that environment, that setting?

Could it be the Boys Club? The Girls Club? Church? The Little League baseball team? School? Will a group of friends provide such feelings and experiences?

Well, sort of. They could help. But what if I add "consistently" to my list of desires for my children? I want my children and grandchildren to feel *consistently* important, valuable, worthwhile, significant, and competent because I believe if they experience those things within their individual self-concept they will be individually healthier people who are going to be better mothers, fathers, husbands, wives, brothers, sisters, friends, church workers, Girl Scout leaders, Little League coaches, teachers, business leaders, chemists, doctors, barbers, and so on—along with a whole host of other roles they will be called upon to perform in their lives.

That is what I want *consistently* for my family members! Wait, what word did I just write? *Family?* That's it! The family is the place where the most important things happen. It is in the family where a person can feel individually important, worthwhile, significant, valuable, and competent with the most consistency.

When that idea set its sights on me and locked on its radar, I was done in! I knew the family was the best place for this to happen and I desperately wanted it to happen within the heart and soul of each of my family members.

So, how does a healthy family work? Could I figure it out? I decided to try. I checked the local libraries and bookstores and found next to nothing on healthy and functional families. There was a lot about dysfunctional families, but that was it. It took me a few years to identify what I thought the basic elements and building blocks of a healthy, functional family were. I then took some time to test out my thinking and ideas with lots of people to see if my conclusions were valid. I found that at least two things must happen in every family: (1) the parents must actively parent and (2) the parents must be willing to look at themselves from time to time and evaluate their situation, being willing to change if needed.

So, let me start you—the parent—out with something active so you can feel immediately involved. The following short survey will ask you some very fundamental questions about the core ideas presented in the book. Take this survey both now and then again when you finish reading the book. See if anything changes. Here goes.

THE FAMILY SURVEY

On a scale of one to ten, evaluate the following areas of your family life.

The general atmosphere in my home and family is what I want it to be.

No (0)_____Yes (10)

My children are learning and growing to my satisfaction.

No (0)_____Yes (10)

I am content with my own involvement in and commitment to my family.

No (0)_____Yes (10)

I know how to create desired changes in my family.

No (0)_____Yes (10)

My spouse and I are working together to create the kind of family we want.

No (0)_____Yes (10)

The communication in our family is good and effective.

No (0)_____Yes (10)

I know how to teach my children to be the kind of people they (and I) would like them to be.

No (0)_____Yes (10)

My relationships within the family are what I would like them to be.

No (0)_____Yes (10)

I am satisfied with how my family is turning out.

No (0)_____Yes (10)

We have a good time and lots of fun and enjoyment in our family.

No (0)_____Yes (10)

I hope those questions got you thinking. As you read, you'll find that thinking is actually a very big part of being a parent.

After my mother passed away just short of age ninety-two, I went through a number of her things. By most standards she had very little. However, I found she had kept virtually every family letter, every family picture, and every item you could imagine related to her large extended family. She kept nothing else. What she chose to keep impressed me. After ninety-two years of living, she kept "family stuff" and that was about it. I think my mother had figured out something that can teach all of us a very important lesson. The lesson: When you get to the end of your life journey, it will be your *family* stuff that matters most.

When I was a much younger father, I put our four oldest boys in the bathtub together one evening. They were all under the age of seven. They were young and rambunctious. They loved to take baths together, but I had told them to be careful not to splash water on the floor. Right. I was in the bedroom and could hear the action picking up. More laughter. More noise. More splashing. Then I heard a big splash and lots of water exiting the tub. I ran into the bathroom and, sure enough, the floor was covered with water. I started to get after my boys but saw smiles all over their faces—along with lots of water. You've seen the typical flooded bathroom scene. Most every parent has seen it many times over.

The parent–child relationship within the family is a unique relationship that cannot truly be replicated.

For some reason, rather than resorting to my usual anger, I stopped and reminded them to be careful not to splash. Telling that to little boys is like telling someone not to breathe! I walked out of the bathroom and sat back down on my bed. I remember thinking how wonderful it was that those little boys could be having so much fun together—even at the expense of our bathroom floor! I remember thinking how fortunate I was to be their dad and how glad I was that we were a family with love in our family relationships. After thinking that, I went in search of a mop to clean up the floor! Those four little boys are now thirty-five, thirty-four, thirty-three, and thirty-one and still having fun together.

The family is a *one-of-a-kind* way to raise children and help them become healthy adults. The parent-child relationship within the family is a unique relationship that cannot truly be replicated. This relationship has potential like no other. The need for belonging and love can be fulfilled in the family in a way that a baseball team or a bridge club will never match. This is a *family*. Love in the family is unlike love anywhere else. Learning in the family is unlike learning anywhere else. Service in the family is unlike service anywhere else. This is because of who we are in relation to the other members of the family. We must protect this unique relationship setting called the family.

I will never forget a very simple and yet profound sentence from a young university student's paper some years ago. I kept this sentence in my personal journal so I would not forget it: "My family has been the greatest influence in my life in helping me to become the person that I have always wanted to be. I have never doubted my own significance in this world because of my family." I remember reading that sentence and wondering for quite some time what type of influence I was on my family.

What type of influence are you? I'd like you to answer that question as you read this book. To help you find the answer, grab a notebook to keep with you as you read. Think of it as your *family project notebook*. Write down your thoughts and impressions as you read the book. Perhaps you can use the notebook to take the personal evaluations included in each chapter. I've found that writing something down makes it more meaningful and makes me more likely to take action. See if the same works for you.

THE PURPOSE OF FAMILIES

Why do we have families? How do they work? How do you assess where your own family stands? How do you improve? Our world today is full of people running to and fro, frantically looking for a place to find happiness, peace, and stability—a place of rest from busy and complex lives. They are looking for a safe haven where they can regain their strength. They are looking for a place that sustains them, a place where they are not alone. *That place is the family.*

As a society, we need to protect and build the family. Too often in the world today, so-called families are really just loose-knit groups whose members stop only to eat, do the wash, sleep, and occasionally interact a little. As we swiftly pass by each other, we barely acknowledge one another. Nothing very significant transpires among us. Startling data backs up what many of you observe just by looking at your neighbors or your own families. This data indicates that many of our families never get to be official families, and far too many don't last as families once they get started. Recent statistics indicate that one-third of infants born in the United States are born out of wedlock. And more than half of all marriages end in divorce (Linda J. Waite and Maggie Gallagher, *The Case for Marriage* [Garden City, N.Y.: Doubleday, 2000], 187).

The certain embrace of the family makes facing complex challenges in life so much more tolerable. It allows those challenges to improve us rather than to crush us.

These struggling families, as well as those that are considered healthy and functional, are at the foundation of our society. Every person in society came from a family and brings what he learned there to his profession, his public service, his own family, and, really, the world at large. That is why the family ideally must be about teaching, learning, loving, nurturing, caring, giving, sacrificing, helping, guiding, playing, laughing, and facing challenges together. It should be about relationships, interpersonal commitments, tolerance, and forgiveness. For both children and parents, it should be about growing up. Growing up includes many moments of *not* measuring up, moments which threaten the self-esteem of both parents and children. Growing up brings moments of uncertainty for family members. That is normal. You can expect it. But it is important to face moments of uncertainty while embraced by others in the family. The certain embrace of the family makes facing complex challenges in life so much more tolerable. It allows those challenges to improve us rather than to crush us. The family is a stabilizing force in the midst of our challenges.

As you learn about the functional family in this book, you will see that I have tried to blend the ideal and the real. Some of what you read may seem too ideal, so please keep in mind that the ideal is merely something that shows the way. It is unlikely that any of us is at an ideal place in relation to the characteristics of the more functional family. It is my hope that the principles in this book will encourage you to move toward the ideal rather than feel defeated by it. Ideal perceptions of the family can be inspiring.

A very busy person I know, after reading some of the suggestions in later chapters of this book, was in his den working on a project one evening at dinnertime. His wife sent their four-year-old son to tell him dinner was ready. The little boy called him to dinner and turned to go back down the stairs to the kitchen. His father, struck by a moment of opportunity, stopped him and sat him on his lap. He said to him, "I am so glad you did what Mommy asked and came to call me to dinner. And I am very happy that *you* are the one who came to get me. After we eat, would you play a game with me?" His little son beamed and agreed to play a game with his dad after dinner. Holding hands, they went down to the kitchen together. My friend told me that the most significant thing about the experience was the realization of how easy it is to have a positive influence in your child's life. You just need to be aware of how important it is.

Ultimately, all the growing and overcoming that life requires of us can strengthen our sense of self-respect and self-esteem. It can also disrupt that sense. Whether you experience one or the other can be a direct outgrowth of the love and guidance available in the family. Family work can, therefore, be demanding and require much of all its members. It can even feel like a burden at times. That is understandable. There are ways to lift some of those burdens as the sustaining arms available to us in the family hold and strengthen us. Some of the arms may not be very strong all of the time, but they do their part, and the joint effort somehow works.

COMMITMENT

At its core, the success of the family is based on the commitment of its members. In today's world, however, commitments are quite easily broken and often dismissed. The family has the potential to be a place where we will not permit that to happen. The blood that flows in the veins of the family is commitment. What are the evidences of your commitment to your family right now? Families need to be trustworthy and dependable. One of my favorite statements is this: "No other success can compensate for failure in the home" (James Edward McCulloch, *Home: The Savior of Civilization* [Washington, D.C.: Southern Co-Operative League, 1924], 42). I believe that those who minimize the importance of the family will come to deeply regret it.

At the heart of my work with the family is a plea to put the family at the top of your list of priorities—above careers, hobbies, and other personal interests. I want you to actively work at making the family a very special part of your life. I hope that by asking yourself some potentially challenging questions as you read each chapter you will find some good ideas on how to work with your family and be a positive influence in your children's lives.

Some time back, my wife, Sherri, and I decided that we really wanted to get our extended family together once a month for what I call a "Family Evening." We sent emails explaining what we wanted to do and why. Many in the family thought it was a good idea, but everyone was busy and had their own lives to lead.

Finally, after much effort, we pulled it off. We held our first extended Family Evening. We held it at our house and it included an activity for the little ones and a discussion for the adults. The children's part went great. The adults' part was not as satisfying. The children were in and out, causing disturbances so we could not really talk together—too many distractions. We considered it a mild success, but the enthusiasm was minimal and another such evening was not held for quite a while. But we did not give up.

At its core, the success of the family is based on the commitment of its members.

Some months later we arranged another extended Family Evening at our oldest son's home. He has a great play area upstairs, out of the way, for the kids. After our family dinner, we sent the kids upstairs to play. (This is typically all they really want to do anyway!) Meanwhile we had a wonderful adult discussion downstairs in the big family room. Everyone seemed to enjoy being together as we discussed how to maintain good adult relationships in our family when we were all so busy and had such complex lives with children, work, school, and so on. It was very productive and we enjoyed being together. It was successful enough that we continue to hold these get-togethers at our son's home on the last Sunday of each month. Following birth order, each of our children and his or her spouse, if married, lead the discussion for that month. The discussion can revolve around anything they would like to share that they feel would benefit us in our family life together. We could have given up. We didn't. It was discouraging at times trying to get it going. But we did it and are glad that we remained committed to our family.

Often during family get-togethers, I just sit back and observe my own children, those who have married into our family, and my grandchildren. At times I feel very emotionally touched by the scene before me. These are "my people." I receive a lot from them and I also want to give to them. Looking at them and feeling the uniquely powerful feeling of family generally sends me on a soul-searching trip to find out what I should work on to be a good father and grandfather in my family. I think about such things a lot. I hope you do too.

WHO HAS THE ULTIMATE RESPONSIBILITY FOR THE FAMILY?

If commitment in family relationships is a must, it follows that this important question also be answered: Who is ultimately responsible for establishing and nurturing the spirit of commitment and trust in the family? Knowing the answer to this question is key to understanding how a healthy family functions. *The major responsibility for how the family functions belongs to the parents.* You can describe the successful elements of any organization, but if you fail to identify who the leaders are, and thus who is ultimately responsible, then its goals and objectives may not be achieved. The leaders in the family are the parents. You are the *family directors.*

The leaders in the family are the parents. You are the family directors.

In the long run, there are few things that need to be maintained with greater permanence than the family. We must find ways to nurture its strength, which will build a foundation for the permanence of each family. One of my adult children said this to me about her own responsibility as a parent: "I don't want to just hope I know what to do as a parent. I want to be *sure* I know what to do as a parent."

PUTTING THE FAMILY FIRST

I have always admired people who choose to put the family first. I have a feeling that they will ultimately be happy with that decision. About fifteen years ago, when our twin daughters, Lindi and Lori, were guards on the junior high school basketball team, they brought home their game schedule. All of their games were to be played on weekdays at 3 P.M.! No! Not during the afternoon! How could I, their dad, ever get there to watch them play? I wanted them to know I loved them and was thrilled that they could play. Getting to play was quite a big deal, considering that they were 4' 10" and 5' 1", respectively. I went to my office and looked at my teaching and counseling schedule. I always had busy afternoons. But I went to work and changed my schedule on game days to allow me to be there for at least some of each game.

It was quite an experience the first day I showed up and sat in the stands with Sherri and a bunch of screaming junior high students. Lindi and Lori were warming up and looked up in the stands to find us. They gave us a big smile and wave. For me, the moment was priceless. I had so wanted to be there for them.

I recognize that this is not possible for many parents. My reason for telling the story is to illustrate a principle rather than an expectation. The principle is that caring, sacrifice, and commitment must be evident in family life. Maybe you can't change your work schedule, but you can change something. And it is the change that sends a message. Sherri and I once heard our son Paul give an address on families in which he said something we liked: "Children need to be committed *to*."

Your commitment *to your children* needs to be crystal clear. Show it however you can. You might not be able to attend every game, but you can make a phone call, send a card, or take the time to talk about the game.

Putting the family first in life is a decision. It is a matter of priorities. It is not that other things in life are unimportant; they may simply be *less* important. I have spent a long professional career talking with people who wrestled with the place of the family in their day-to-day living. They commonly put other things first. Business success, hobbies and pastimes, fun, earning money, and other personal pursuits took most of their time and interest. The years passed and they felt empty. They were dissatisfied. Ultimately they were shocked to realize that far too often they had set aside the things that mattered most in the long run, and time had run out.

A clear commitment to the family requires dedicated work. It is not short-term. Children need to come first much of the time. And that requires sacrifices on the parents' part. That is something many parents I see wrestle with. It's okay to wrestle with it, but do so and then come to a firm conclusion about what you do in life as a parent so that you won't do it begrudgingly. There is no higher human privilege than giving from your heart to your family. That privilege is even more meaningful and significant when you are doing your parenting in a difficult situation where children and parents struggle.

Now, don't think that I'm advocating that you drop all other significant and important commitments in life. Legitimately, life has other important aspects to it besides the family. For some, outside-the-family ventures are rejuvenating and provide a much-needed a break. We all need a break! Take it. But keep the family first. After all, home is where the most important things happen.

SINGLE PARENTS

I know some of you are single parents. In many ways, your challenge is greater. I admire your hard work and how much you care about your children. You don't get applauded often enough. It is very hard to do by yourself. There is little relief. My mother was a single parent for many years, and I know how hard it was for her. I was her youngest child during that time, so I watched her work at it alone. She had many challenges. I hope I have written this book in a way that is sensitive to single parents and helpful to them and to all parents. The principles are the same for all parents, but implementing them when you are alone is much more challenging. I hope this book gives you some good ideas and encouragement.

I encourage you who are single parents to identify other single parents with whom you can work. Choose carefully, of course. You want healthy relationships. I hope you will find other families with whom you can associate who have time for you and interest in you. Perhaps they can take your children every so often so you can have some time alone to get a break from your awesome responsibilities. Families, look for single parents who can benefit from your help. Perhaps your children and theirs can play together. Invite them to join with you from time to time for a Family Evening or other joint get-togethers. I believe all of us should reach out and help single parents who may need help in carrying their heavy responsibilities. Too many people in this world are called upon to go it alone.

I am also aware that there may be two-parent homes where one parent is highly interested in family matters and the other may be hard to involve. Perhaps this book will help the parent who lacks interest or feels that all the work won't matter. But there are many families where one parent is called upon to carry the major challenges of parenting alone. Hopefully the family life concepts here will help you do just that. You can do the brainstorming and planning yourself or team up with another interested parent who may have a similar situation. Don't lose hope. It can still be done. Keep reading. I am not trying to put blame on the less-involved parent. Why one parent chooses not to invest in such an effort is often complex. He or she may just be discouraged or feel these "self-help family projects" are a waste of time. Try not to put your energy into blaming anyone. Just go to work and see what you can do yourself. Maybe your partner will like what you are doing and occasionally ask if you need some help. You never know. Blaming drains life energy out of you. Leave it alone.

THE PARENTS' RELATIONSHIP

A runner with a big race ahead knows that physical conditioning is key to success in the race. As you consider the arduous task you face as parents in directing a family, ask yourself what lies at the foundation of your day-to-day family work. You'll find that it is the *relationship* of the two parents. Your relationship must be as healthy and functional as possible, or else you will have trouble working together to increase family health and well-being. The health and ultimate success of the parental relationship depends on two things more than anything else: humility and selflessness on the part of both parents. Each of you needs to recognize the importance of putting yourself aside in the name of the larger objective—family well-being. A unified commitment to the family needs to be obvious.

The job of directing a family is significantly harder if the parents do not possess sufficient humility and selflessness. When humility and selflessness combine in a parent, it is breathtaking and has a great influence on the overall family. It is also important that the parents *like each other* in spite of idiosyncrasies and weaknesses. They also need to have open and honest communication with each other. Obviously, to pull all this off, you have to be able to work together. Parents must *seek* to know how they affect each other. If you present a personal barrier to your spouse that affects how you work together as parents, you need to face it. Don't wait for someone to point it out to you. Try to find out about yourself as a spouse and parent. Every so often I ask my wife, "What is it like to be married to me?" That takes courage.

The health and ultimate success of the parental relationship depends on two things more than anything else: humility and selflessness on the part of both parents.

You must want to do much more than merely cope with your parenting responsibilities. The goal is not just to survive but to thrive—although there are days when surviving is definitely a short-term objective! You must actively work to exhibit real commitment to the work of the family. Is it hard work? Often, yes. Can it be deeply satisfying, even to tired parents? It can be. Please keep reading.

WHAT DO YOU WANT IN YOUR FAMILY?

You may struggle with a variety of complex emotions over the condition of your family. Or you may see the influence you are having on your family and wonder if it is as positive as it should be. Or you might be depressed and discouraged over the impact of your spouse on your family, and you wish you knew how to help him or her understand that impact.

What matters is that you want to improve. You want to know

how you can do better with your children than you are doing now. The deepest and most heartfelt human desires I have ever seen seem to manifest themselves in things that relate to family and children. At times, the pursuit of a good, solid family seems to produce feelings of despair and discouragement. Often those feelings simply mean that we care.

Let me just say something to *very discouraged* parents here. Is there a solution for you? This whole book is for you, of course. Please read it carefully and keep in mind the *ten-scale*. Pretty much everything we talk about in this book will be evaluated by using a ten-scale. As you learn more about the scale, you'll find that it will keep you away from black/white and either/or thinking. You will learn to consider your family's characteristics by thinking of them in *degrees* rather than being in a state of all or nothing. The message for you in the ten-scale process is that change and improvement occur in *steps* and *stages*. If I could make one suggestion to you in this first chapter, I would say jump ahead and read chapter 8 on relationships right now. When families struggle and the whole "solution" looks bigger than you are, there is one place you can always work—and that is on *relationships*. You make whatever contribution you can, in small or large ways, to various relationships in the family.

Some of you might feel you have a basically good family but want it to be better. You have a feeling that there are some things that might really get your family to "hum" and achieve a level of well-being that you do not now enjoy. This book is for any family, whether that family is in a fair amount of trouble or just wants to step up a few notches. What I ask of you will require that you be open and honest in looking at yourself as a parent. Undoubtedly, you will discover strong points in yourself as well as some areas that need work. Once you understand the inner workings of your family, you can assess them and then see if *you*, as the parent, need to approach your family differently.

In 1993, one of our sons was getting ready to go to Chile for a couple of years. I was going out of the area on a professional speaking assignment, so I asked him to go with me. It would be two years before we would see each other again. While we were driving the three hundred miles to my speaking assignment, I asked him if he would mind telling me what it was like to grow up in our family with me as the dad. I listened to him for quite some time as he explained to me what he thought about my question. He asked me what it was like for me to grow up in the family I came from. So we each shared our family experiences and we learned something from each other. I certainly learned some things about myself as a dad—pros and cons. We can learn from our children if we are willing to be the students from time to time. As you read this book you will find plenty of ideas and ways to do just that. The one thing you'll see me advocating most is the idea that holding regular discussions with your spouse about the well-being of your family can make all the difference—and it can take as little as thirty minutes a week.

FAMILY DISCUSSION TIME

I have talked to many committed parents who struggle with how to "get it done" when it comes to good parenting. Family Discussion Time will help you do that. I highly recommend it. What is it? It is a specific time set aside each week when you as parents take time to talk together about your family. It is a time to talk about what you are trying to accomplish as parents. It should last about thirty minutes or so. This meeting is just for the parents. That's it. Simple. Crucial. It makes *all* the difference.

So, stop everything! Set aside a specific time each week that will be called *Family Discussion Time (FDT)*. It could be Monday night at 9 P.M. Or Sunday morning at 10 A.M. The day and time don't matter. What does is that you do it as regularly as you possibly can. Seek an uninterrupted, private time and setting so you can concentrate fully on the needs of your family. Make notes on what you talk about so that the next time you meet you can talk about what you intended to do and see how it went.

There is only *one* topic to consider during Family Discussion Time: *the condition and needs of your family*. Remember, the needs of your family will include *your* needs as parents. Don't forget those. If it works well, at the conclusion of your Family Discussion Time you should have written down or have clear in your mind, depending on your personal style, the answers to who, what, where, and when as they relate to family matters you intend to work on. Please do not assume that once you talk over a family issue that it is done. Family Discussion Time must be aimed at how to incorporate your plans into your family life. You may want to agree that expanding the conversation to include some of the children on a particular topic may be a good idea. In some instances, your children can help you figure out how to implement your plans and thinking into daily family life. This will also help them learn how to do it, so they can pursue the same approach when they are parents. This is what I call *family modeling*, and it can have a multigenerational effect.

TWO MORE KEY FAMILY MEETINGS

Along with Family Discussion Time come two other valuable meetings: *Family Evening* and *Family Council*. Family Evening involves regularly setting aside an hour or two one evening *each week* for the family to be together. The evening can begin with a short learning experience followed by a fun activity and some treats. It can be any evening in the week, but it works best if it is the same evening each week so everyone can plan on it. Family Council is held as needed for the purpose of specific problem solving—such as planning a trip or discussing how to handle something, like teasing or fighting, in the family. By holding these three family meetings you are showing your children how to live and how to run a family. These meetings are used by families that work *together*. And these important family meetings create traditions of security in the family. They help family members build confidence in their ability to solve problems and face challenges together.

A PERSONAL PERSPECTIVE

I remember a night many years ago when I had trouble sleeping. I got out of bed and sat on our living room couch, gazing out the large window in the front of our home. As I had done many times before, I thought about my family. I wondered if I was doing a good job as a father and a husband. I was concerned about both. I remember wondering what I needed to do differently. I wondered if I was too self-critical in this part of my life. I questioned if there really were something I needed to do differently to strengthen my family. There was *nothing* that mattered to me more than the other eleven people who were at that moment asleep in my home.

Being a parent is both the hardest and the most wonderful thing you will ever do in life.

Much of the thinking I did that night and the hard problem solving I have done since have influenced what I have written in this book. I really wanted *my* home to be a place where family members felt valued, encouraged, and loved, and where they could learn how to live well. I wanted it to be a place where each one could grow, develop, laugh, play, and hug. I hoped it would be a place where they could make mistakes and feel someone was there to listen to them, help them, teach them, and set a good example for them. I did not want them to feel I devalued them because they struggled. I wanted our home to be a place that, when the time came to leave and head out on their own, they would miss it a little and want to come back to it with their own children. I wanted each one to say they came to know service, caring about others, kindness, faith, gratitude, and thoughtfulness better because they lived in our home and were part of our family. That is what I thought about that night . . . and many nights since. Even in the ups and downs of what I have done as a parent, I hoped my children would see me as someone who worked hard at it because I loved them.

Being a parent is both the hardest and the most wonderful thing I have ever done in my life. Knowing how challenging it is, I would still go back and do it all over again. It has challenged me and made me a better person. It has exposed my weaknesses and inadequacies—I have felt very discouraged at times—but have been able to draw on my firm commitment to my family to see me through those hard times. I felt that if I could quit, then any parent could quit. *Quit* was not a word in my parenting vocabulary. *Committed* was. If living fifty-eight years has taught me anything, it is that the most important decisions I will ever make in my life are those related to my family.

CHAPTER 2

FamilyThink–A Key Family Concept

I am known among my colleagues and even my family members as "the guy with the yellow pad of paper." I think by writing down thoughts, feelings, and questions on my yellow pad of paper. I keep it right by my computer in my office, and when I have thoughts about my family I write them on it. If I want to spend time later thinking about one of my children, I write that on my yellow pad of paper. I love my yellow pad of paper! Sometimes I do family problem solving on it. I will write something like, "What can I do to help _____?" Or, "How can we have better Family Evenings?" That way I don't forget what I need to think about later when it comes to my family. It is a somewhat informal way of evaluating things that have to do with my family. Sometimes I will thumb through four or five pages of things I have jotted down over a few weeks' period of time and ponder where my "family thinking" has taken me during that period of time. That keeps me on my "family toes."

FamilyThink—looking at yourself and your family and really thinking about what you are doing—is at the heart of what healthy families do. Such evaluation leads to *family thinking.* It helps families become what they want to become as a group and as individuals. A family member can do self-evaluations, and families as a group can do family evaluations. Professionally, I've found that FamilyThink is a big deal in functional families. Some families are fairly formal about it; others do their FamilyThinking "in their heads." Of course, if you fear evaluation and what it might uncover, it will be difficult to FamilyThink. But if you change your focus and concentrate on what evaluation can help you and your family become, you'll find that FamilyThink really isn't all that hard. Think of athletic teams, businesses, humanitarian groups, Scouting organizations, parent-teacher-student groups, or any other group with a purpose. How well do they do if they do not look at themselves on a regular basis?

> *FamilyThink—looking at yourself and your family and really thinking about what you are doing—is at the heart of what healthy families do.*

EVALUATION BY DEGREES

The health of your family can be best understood by assessing various types of family characteristics *by degree.* To help you do that, I invite you to actively participate in thinking about and determining how you influence your family. Self-evaluation and related family evaluation can be done in simple ways. Use the ten-scale (rating on a scale of one to ten) to help you evaluate each area.

Undoubtedly, every family falls short of being perfect. Knowing that always makes me feel better. Knowing my own family's relation to the ideal helps me work harder to get there.

All of us struggle with ups and downs in family life. We have stronger and weaker areas in our family living. That is normal. In this chapter, you will get to answer some thought-provoking questions about yourself as *an influence* in your family and about *your family* itself. I invite you to really dig into yourself and attempt to understand yourself in relation to your family. This can be an eye-opening and inspiring experience. As you start to FamilyThink, you may also want to jot down the thoughts and ideas that come to you regarding your family. This is what that yellow notepad is for. Of course, some of you may not want to do the more formal FamilyThink assessments recommended in this book. They aren't "your style." That is fine. Just read the introspective questions given to help you think about your family from different angles. If you like more formal assessments, then you will really like what follows. Enjoy!

THE TEN-SCALE

The ten-scale involves ranking items from 1 to 10. A high number on the ten-scale means you demonstrate a high level or degree of whatever characteristic you are considering. A low number means you demonstrate less of that characteristic. Whether you are considering a positive or a negative characteristic does not matter; a high number always means a higher level or amount and a low number always means a lower level or amount. Here is an illustration: Ask yourself a question, such as, "Am I physically present and psychologically available to my family as a parent?" Now evaluate yourself with a number between 1 and 10 (a ten-scale assessment). A high number, such as 7 or 8, indicates that you have demonstrated a real interest in your family. You make decisions to put aside other interests to be with them. You intentionally involve yourself in family activities such as reading to your children, playing with them, or talking with them. A low number, such as 2 or 3, says that you are not very involved. You are just not present to do much for your family. Or it could mean you are there but not "really" there. You may be into other activities that take your mind and heart away from your family. Ten-scale numbers are intended only to give you an idea regarding where you feel you are in an area of concern to you. Your assessments give you a place to begin or refine your thinking. If you feel particularly courageous, ask a friend or your spouse to evaluate you. Comparing ten-scale evaluations is invaluable. If your observations differ from those of your spouse or friend, a chat with that person about the differences may be helpful. Remember, such assessments are just a group of subjective opinions that can potentially help you think more and do more for your family.

PERSONAL EVALUATION

A valuable type of self-examination is looking at the chief characteristics you exhibit as a parent. I recall counseling a couple who were struggling with their relationships with their children. I asked them, "What do you want to be like in your family and in your relationships with your children?" They each looked at me with a big question mark on their faces. My question was obviously perplexing. I clarified: "What are the central characteristics you want to convey to your children? How do you want your children to view you as parents?" The father ended up saying, "Fun, confident, and a good example." The mother said, "Accepting, loving, and available." I did my usual ten-scale activity and asked them to rate themselves for each of those characteristics. The dad said, "1, 5, and 5." The mom said "5, 4, and 7." We had an interesting conversation about how satisfied they were with those self-evaluations. We also discussed how they could improve some of those characteristics in the near future. Self-evaluation can tell you so much about yourself. It helps you know where you are, which serves as a basis for determining where you might choose to go from there. In this case, the dad, recognizing himself as a 1 on being fun in the family, decided to try two things: to play informally with his kids more and to be more actively jovial around the house. He said he had been pretty uninvolved and fairly boring. He was willing to take on those changes and ultimately move his self-assessment from 1 to 5 in the area of being more fun to be around at home.

The mom recognized her self-evaluation in the areas of accepting and loving were 5 and 4—not good enough, in her opinion. She acknowledged she was quite a critical parent too much of the time. She felt she needed to take more opportunities to give physical love through hugs, kisses, holding hands during walks—actions that included wholesome physical touching—and also to give more compliments rather than just pointing out mistakes. She thought by paying attention to those things she could raise her self-assessment scores in those two areas by a couple of points, which would make a big difference in how she wanted to be as a mother.

If you really want to take this seriously, get out your notebook and do a special "self-evaluation project" for a month. Try following these steps: (1) identify an area of concern that you want to evaluate and work on (it could come from the topics of the chapters in this book); (2) do a self-evaluation on that particular area of concern using a ten-scale and some written descriptive comments on how you see the situation; (3) consider this self-evaluation thoughtfully during your regular Family Discussion Time by talking about your self-evaluation and how you and your spouse view it; (4) establish a short-term plan to achieve some improvements and subsequent growth in the area of concern; (5) take a week or two to work your plan; and then (6) come back to Family Discussion Time and talk about what happened. The key is *doing* those six steps or something similar to them. *Thinking* about them helps, but *doing* them helps much more.

Be patient. Just work at it. Sometimes things will go well and produce desirable outcomes. Other times the outcomes won't be as desirable. The most important thing is that you do it and keep doing it, accruing large or small amounts of success from time to time, but always trying to help your family. Even if you achieve only half your short-term goal, that's good. If you had never set the goal in the first place, you might not have changed anything in that specific area.

Of course, sometimes life just gets in the way, even when we, as parents, are consciously working toward positive results in our families. There are reasons for this. Some days you can be proud of yourself for just coping. Allow for those tough days. On other days you may wish you could have someone who knows about families move in with you, sit and take notes, and give you some help on ways to improve. Actually, you can do that evaluation yourself through use of the ten-scale. It is your own assessment. It gives you a way to look at yourself and your family.

The great thing about this approach is that *you* are making something happen in your family. *You* are working on and thinking about your family. *You* are acting in behalf of your family. *You are being active, not passive.* This personal effort is essential in this active approach to family development. FamilyThink helps you significantly in your important role as parent and family leader.

So, let's move on to the first step in your quest to better know yourself as a parent. What follows is a parental self-evaluation. Complete it using the ten-scale concept. You can do the various self-evaluations in your family project notebook, taking time to answer the questions that follow each number, or you can fill out the evaluations right in the book. All through the pages of this book are numerous interesting opportunities to do other informal evaluations. One person who read a version of this manuscript prior to its going to print wrote numbers right in the text all through the book, evaluating herself in many different places. Could be fun—and eye-opening too!

PERSONAL SELF-ASSESSMENT

Rate yourself on a scale of 1 (not true of you) to 10 (extremely true of you).

I am a lot like my father._____

Brief explanation:

Effect on my current family:

I am a lot like my mother._____

Brief explanation:

Effect on my current family:

I have high expectations._____

Brief explanation:

Effect on my current family:

I am a perfectionist._____

Brief explanation:

Effect on my current family:

I criticize and grow angry easily._____

Brief explanation:

Effect on my current family:

I organize well._____

Brief explanation:

Effect on my current family:

I am thoughtful and sensitive._____

Brief explanation:

Effect on my current family:

I respect the opinions of others._____

Brief explanation:

Effect on my current family:

I am sarcastic._____

Brief explanation:

Effect on my current family:

I am loving._____

Brief explanation:

Effect on my current family:

I am good-natured._____

Brief explanation:

Effect on my current family:

I am selfish._____

Brief explanation:

Effect on my current family:

I intimidate others._____

Brief explanation:

Effect on my current family:

I am competitive._____

Brief explanation:

Effect on my current family:

I am generous and giving._____

Brief explanation:

Effect on my current family:

I worry about pleasing others._____

Brief explanation:

Effect on my current family:

I experience a lot of stress and anxiety._____

Brief explanation:

Effect on my current family:

I am depressed._____

Brief explanation:

Effect on my current family:

I am funny._____

Brief explanation:

Effect on my current family:

I am productive._____

Brief explanation:

Effect on my current family:

I work hard._____

Brief explanation:

Effect on my current family:

I am a leader._____

Brief explanation:

Effect on my current family:

I am kind._____

Brief explanation:

Effect on your current family:

I am punitive and harsh._____

Brief explanation:

Effect on your current family:

I am controlling (I seek to manage everyone and everything).
_____

Brief explanation:

Effect on your current family:

I am confrontational._____

Brief explanation:

Effect on my current family:

I have integrity._____

Brief explanation:

Effect on my current family:

I am spiritual._____

Brief explanation:

Effect on my current family:

I am mild._____

Brief explanation:

Effect on my current family:

I am self-centered._____

Brief explanation:

Effect on my current family:

I am loyal._____

Brief explanation:

Effect on my current family:

I am honest._____

Brief explanation:

Effect on my current family:

I respect myself._____

Brief explanation:

Effect on my current family;

I speak with a soft and caring tone of voice._____

Brief explanation:

Effect on my current family:

I show gratitude._____

Brief explanation:

Effect on my current family:

I am patient._____

Brief explanation:

Effect on my current family:

I put off my own needs when it is important to do so._____

Brief explanation:

Effect on my current family:

I am friendly._____

Brief explanation:

Effect on my current family:

I am argumentative._____

Brief explanation:

Effect on my current family:

I am passive._____

Brief explanation:

Effect on my current family:

I am shy._____

Brief explanation:

Effect on my current family:

I am opinionated._____

Brief explanation:

Effect on my current family:

I am stubborn._____

Brief explanation:

Effect on my current family:

I am responsible._____

Brief explanation:

Effect on my current family:

I am approachable (family members feel comfortable coming to me)._____

Brief explanation:

Effect on my current family:

I am thoughtful._____

Brief explanation:

Effect on my current family:

I am forgetful._____

Brief explanation:

Effect on my current family:

I am judgmental._____

Brief explanation:

Effect on my current family:

I am unforgiving._____

Brief explanation:

Effect on my current family:

I am strong-willed._____

Brief explanation:

Effect on my current family:

Once you've completed the ten-scale portion of the evaluation, you might find it helpful to complete the summary portion of the worksheet that follows.

SUMMARY

The question you are really trying to answer is, "What am I like as a parent, and how do I influence my family?"

My three best characteristics are—

1.

2.

3.

What are the effects of those three characteristics on my family?

My three worst characteristics are—

1.

2.

3.

What are the effects of those three characteristics on my family?

    What are the next steps you need to take and why? If you take those steps, what do you anticipate will be different for you and your family? Write your response to these questions in your family project notebook. Share them with your spouse if you are married. Share them with another parent if you are single. Get some feedback and ponder these things.

    I hope you have gained a new perspective on the guiding and directing role of parents in the family and that you have taken the first step in your quest to know yourself as a parent and how you may affect your own family. We will proceed in the next chapter to discuss the nature of less functional families so you can assess those characteristics in your own family. In succeeding chapters, you will learn about the characteristics of more functional families so you can assess the status of those characteristics in your own family, as well.

> *The question you are really trying to answer is, "What am I like as a parent, and how do I influence my family?"*

CHAPTER 3

The Influence of Your Family of Origin

I grew up in a troubled family. Life was very hard. My growing up years challenged me. They left me damaged in some ways. It took me years to find my way out of most of it. To some degree, parts of the damage remain. They always will. But now I feel a lot smarter about things, such as the family, than I might have been had I not gone through such a difficult early life. Though a difficult childhood may destroy some people, it can educate and help develop others, offering important perspective on life. The worst kind of "life pain" is that which produces only pain. If we can learn to take that pain to the next level, then it will have more value. The next level is where pain can eventually help us be smarter, wiser, and more sensitive.

What has the pain of my early family life helped me to learn? Has it ultimately helped me to grow into a wiser person? I hope it has. One of my favorite metaphors is the blackboard metaphor: A child is born, and his caretakers begin to write on his personal blackboard. They write messages about him. Some messages are intentional and many are unintentional. But they can be very powerful. They tell the child about himself. Many negative and destructive messages were written on my blackboard up through my teenage years. As I became an adult I realized that I could either believe and accept the messages as they were or work at making some type of new sense out of them so that I could be in charge of my life rather than letting my past own my future. It took a lot of work, but it was worth it.

The worst kind of "life pain" is that which produces only pain. If we can learn to take that pain to the next level, then it will have more value. The next level is where pain can eventually help us be smarter and wiser.

I remember standing on the sidewalk in front of a friend's house one day as his family packed their car for a family vacation. I also watched as they left. I remember wondering why my family did not go on vacations, and why we were different. I even wondered if there were something wrong with me, and perhaps that was why my parents did not take better care of me. Consequently, as I grew into young adulthood and got married, I really wanted to know how healthier families worked. I started watching other families to learn from them. I was going to figure this one out.

Suppose you have just made a decision to pursue a career in a health profession, possibly to become a medical doctor, a nurse, a chiropractor, or a dietitian. In your enthusiasm you go to the local library and look for good books to read on the subject. You find one called *The Human Body: Major Illnesses.* Would you consider this a book full of valuable knowledge? Or would you say, "I really just need to study the *healthy* human body, the positive aspects of human health. I don't need this book"? My guess is that you would want to know both about illnesses in the human body *and* ways to positively enhance health. Similarly, understanding the problems of families with unhealthy characteristics—illnesses, if you will—is quite important in coming to understand, by contrast, the healthy and prospering family.

So, here we go. Let's spend one chapter learning about some of the characteristics of families that are not functioning very well. They are what I term "less functional." I'd like to take a somewhat different look at the idea of troubled or less functional families. I do this because *all families have their difficulties to some degree.* This just means the family does not measure up—in one area or more—to the ideal standard. Does this sound at all like your family? It sure sounds like mine. This is not to say that all families are secretly in major trouble. By labeling something as "less functional," it simply enables us to look at our own families with increased honesty and openness. As you read on, you'll be asked to look at your family of origin and your current family truthfully, with an honest desire to understand how they function. The intent is not to prompt the discovery that your family is dysfunctional, but to help you determine to *what degree* your family is struggling or not yet working satisfactorily in a variety of important areas.

To understand potentially troublesome areas of family living is a benefit to those in the middle of such difficulties, as well as those who want to avoid such things. You will read about basic types of less functional families and also learn about the personal characteristics of individuals who come from these types of families.

As you do so, consider your own family of origin. Was it less functional (below a 3 or a 4 on a ten-scale)? Was it functional but in need of some improvements here and there (a 5 or 6 on a ten-scale)? Was it functional and healthy (a 7 to 10 on a ten-scale) and thus exhibiting characteristics from which others could learn?

To honestly examine your family of origin, as well as your current family, takes desire. Sometimes it takes honesty and courage, especially if you know the numbers could be low. It also seems to take a certain amount of humility and can even be scary. There were times when I felt I did not want to know where I had come from, kind of like I did not want to know if my body was sick. I did not want to be critical of my family of origin or of my current family. But I knew that I *had* to take an honest look at both in order for my current family to progress as it could. I also owed it to my family members. My family was depending on me to help them have a good family experience. You will be surprised at the benefits of looking at where you came from. Your reason for doing this is not to be judgmental but rather to be educated and learn from your family of origin. After you've done that, take a good look

The family you came from and the examples your parents set greatly influence the way you view things in your current family as a parent.

at your current family in areas of potential challenge and difficulty. Of course, that does not assume that your family is in poor condition. Any learning and understanding will benefit you regardless of how strong or weak your family is. Some very strong families may also find ways to focus their attention on areas that need some fine-tuning.

The family you came from and the examples your parents set greatly influence the way you view things in your current family as a parent. We all come from varying degrees of imperfect families. Remember, the term "less functional" as a descriptor is meant to demonstrate a family's distance from the ideal family. Do not be intimidated or discouraged by what you read in this chapter. The evaluations you'll find here are merely an attempt to define, in varying degrees, the less-than-perfect family experiences we have all had. There are various types of less functional families, and they affect parents differently.

I recommend that you use the ten-scale to evaluate whether your family of origin or your current family can be described by any of the following characteristics present in less functional families. You can evaluate the overall condition of your family of origin as well as your current family by making a very subjective "best guess." This is an attempt to evaluate your "feeling" about the family you came from, as well as the one you are in now. In the evaluations that follow, a low number (0 to 4) means you feel the amount of difficulty or dysfunction in your family was or is low. A higher number (7 to 10) means there were or are many difficulties in your family. Rate your past and current families below according to the general difficulty you sense in them:

Family of Origin_____

Current Family_____

THREE TYPES OF
LESS FUNCTIONAL FAMILIES

Each of the remaining chapters in the book will describe the various characteristics of a functional, developing family. This will provide you with insight into the nature of healthy families. But it is wise to first understand the definitions of a less functional family.

Consider three general categories of less functional families: (1) the unpredictable and insecure family; (2) the highly controlled and dominated, or managed, family; and (3) the chaotic and out-of-control family. First, you will get a brief idea of what goes on in each of these types of families, and then you can use the ten-scale to see if any of them might provide you with a useful perspective on your family of origin or your current family. This is FamilyThink at its best.

You may find that parts of all three less functional families exist in your own family. Or you may discover that one type stands out clearly as the type of family you are in now or the type of family you came from. You may find that your family sounds somewhat like one or more of these but you would only rate the strength of what you find at about five on the ten-scale. This means that the similarity between the definition you are reading and your family is moderate. Take a good look and see what you find. Even if you find just a small resemblance with one or more of these less functional families, that will be good for you to know as you look to the future of your own family. After reading each description, use the ten-scale to evaluate it.

1. The unpredictable and insecure family

The main characteristic reported by people in this type of family is *fear*. Some very unhealthy things go on in this family. There could be alcoholism, drug abuse, or sexual, physical, or emotional abuse. Or there could simply be heavy demands, expectations, and pressures. Emotions are usually intense. There could be excessive anger, for example. Sometimes the heavy negative emotion lies under the surface of the family, but everyone feels it. There could be a lot of destructiveness. Trouble in this family can come out of nowhere. Things can be going along pretty well for a short time and then a big wave of trouble will wash over the family. Feelings of fear and anxiety make up the atmosphere. People in this type of family worry a lot.

These families often include a parent who uses his or her parental power to control the children or spouse. Children feel they have to be ready for trouble because they never know when it will rear its ugly head. Children feel they need to protect themselves emotionally and sometimes even physically. Some children are extra good because that protects them from criticism and harm. The trouble could come twice in one day and then nothing for three days. The *unpredictability* of its arrival is unnerving. One minute, family members seem to be measuring up to the "controller's" demands and the next they are not. Family members experience a lot of worry, anxiety, nervousness, and fretting.

What kind of children come out of such a family? That is a complicated question because the basic nature with which each child is born affects how he or she responds to the family environment. However, children from this type of family are commonly very security-oriented. They may have a high need for control themselves and often are "pleasers," doing anything they can to please those around them. Being a "pleaser" allows them to gain more control over the environment they are in. They have a hard time getting to know and be themselves because they are so busy managing their environment and pleasing others around them to secure personal safety. They exhibit a lot of ongoing anxiety and are often nervous and easily stressed out. They can be very tense. Many smile through their pain until the pain becomes too great, and then they emotionally collapse. Living in this family is hard work and causes some members to be hypervigilant, always watching out for trouble.

Rate your family of origin on the characteristics of the unpredictable and insecure family._____

Rate your current family on the same characteristic._____

What are your thoughts and impressions? Write them in your family project notebook so you can think about them more thoughtfully later and perhaps consider them at Family Discussion Time.

2. The highly controlled and dominated family

Members of this family aim to be whatever the parents have decided the family must be, but the ideal is never achieved to the parents' full satisfaction. There are very high expectations in this family. In fact, the expectations are in the realm of perfection. Little error is tolerated. This family is sometimes known as the *critical family*. Much criticism and judgment exist in family life. Other times, it is known as the *angry family*, and anger is commonly employed as a management tool. Family members feel evaluated, like they never quite measure up to the high expectations in the family. Some call this family *unyielding* and *overbearing*. They need to look good, especially to others. Family image is everything. So the parents are *intense managers* of the children's behavior. How the children *feel* is not the key issue, but how they *act visibly* is crucial. A nearly perfect public family image is required. The self-esteem of the parents rides on the performance of the children, so they point out their children's mistakes and errors quickly and incisively. They dictate to their children; they demand. It feels "tight" because everyone is being watched. Children are expected to smile through all this management. They must hold that nearly perfect public family image together, no matter what.

Children in this family likewise worry a lot. They worry about meeting all those expectations without error. They are often preoccupied with being "at the top." They tend to feel pressure even when pressure is not intended. Pressure to perform may become self-imposed to reduce the possibility of failure and parental disapproval. One of the most common responses of children in this type of family is the inability to relax. Children in this family can be very successful as they meet these incredibly high standards.

When they succeed, it is often hard to recognize the pain and difficulties under the surface of their successful lives.

Children who try this hard may eventually succumb to the pressure. They may quit trying at all, because the pressure is too great and they can't take it. They know they will disappoint their perfectionistic parents. Once the "let-down" occurs, they can finally relax because they have broken the cycle.

The parents in this family do a lot of demanding through emotional attempts to control. Their attempts often work, but at a very high price to the children. Commonly, they produce a public child who succeeds and a private child who is exhausted and uptight. This family works so hard to protect its public image that the contrived image often does not seem real. Family members feel like they are play-acting a script that has been handed to them. The instructions are not to miss a word and to follow the script flawlessly, no matter how they feel. In this family children often perceive their parents as being chronically disappointed in them.

Rate your family of origin on the characteristics of the highly controlled and dominated family._____

Rate your current family on this family characteristic._____

What are your thoughts and impressions? Again, write your impressions in your family notebook so you can think about them later.

3. The chaotic and out-of-control family

The main characteristics here are *confusion* and *lack of guidance*. Very little is defined and not much clear guidance is given in this family. There are no set times for anything. Family members can't count on anyone within the family. Will someone show up to take you to school? Who knows? Will someone show up at your baseball game or piano concert? Who knows? Someone might, but it will be late, maybe quite late. Are there rules? Maybe and maybe not. If so, they will be dealt with inconsistently. Family life is very unpredictable. Dinner at six? Who knows? Clean clothes, clean house? Who knows? Someone to help you with your homework? Can't be sure. Lots of noise? Possibly. There is a lot of chaotic energy around the home, and it feels out of control. Discipline by the parents is doubtful, but it is inconsistent if there is any. One minute the discipline is really tough and the next nonexistent. Feels pretty shaky.

Children recognize that there is little definition of what their family is and represents and will either work hard to produce more control or spin out of emotional control themselves. They may also grow up hypervigilant, watching everyone and everything so as to anticipate trouble and chaos. They hope they can find a way to stabilize things. They will often leave the chaotic environment and try to find one that is more predictable. Sometimes they just give up and drown in the chaos. They feel very insecure because of the unpredictable nature of such chaos, and they just don't know if their needs will ever be met. They are confused about how things in the family ought to be. Sometimes the chaos and unpredictability are a product of the parents being absent too much. It is not surprising that children try to find what is missing in the family by going outside the family, often to unhealthy relationships based upon violations of family standards.

Rate your family of origin on the characteristics of the chaotic and out-of-control family._____

Rate your current family on this family characteristic._____

What are your thoughts and impressions? Yep, put them in your family notebook. Lots to think about later!

WHAT ARE PEOPLE LIKE WHO COME FROM THESE FAMILIES?

Think back to that book you found in the local library on human health and illness. Once you learn about the basic causes of poor human health, you then need to know the *symptoms* of a sick human body, right? The next section will help you understand what people who come from less functional families are like. The *degree* to which a family is less functional has something to do with the degree to which these troubled characteristics appear in the lives of the family members.

There are many variations of the three general categories of less functional families just defined. Your family may be a slight variation. Some may experience a mix of all three. The characteristics of people from such families still remain essentially the same. Each one will be described. Your job will be to do a ten-scale assessment on each one to see if you are experiencing it in your own personal life, or if you notice it in the personal characteristics of your children. Our three types of less functional families do *not* always produce all the characteristics that will be discussed in the remainder of this chapter, but there is a strong likelihood that *some* of these characteristics will, in varying degrees, become a part of the children who come out of such less functional families.

TYPICAL CHARACTERISTICS OF INDIVIDUALS FROM LESS FUNCTIONAL FAMILIES

Let's look now at the specific characteristics of people who come from less functional families.

1. Generalized fear and anxiety

All three groups of families produce a fear in members that they won't measure up, that they won't know what to do when caught in a serious trouble spot. They fear there won't be enough help, that they are not good enough, that they are not loved enough, or that they are not valuable enough. They are anxious about not adequately meeting expectations; they worry that important personal needs won't be met, and on and on. Their lack of self-confidence affects how they perceive people and things around them. They may carry this burden with them their whole lives unless they get some type of help. It all rolls into a confusing mass of general anxiety and apprehension. They *know* there is trouble out there—a lot of it—and they feel that they must *always* be ready for it, or it may get them.

Rate this personal characteristic here._____

Also rate each child in your family here._____ _____

_____ _____ _____

2. A feeling that love is highly conditional and limited in quantity

Love to the human spirit is like water to the body. It is essential. A person *must* have it for the human spirit to thrive. Love tells someone that he is good, important, and valuable. People who feel that love is conditional or limited typically believe that *if* love ever came their way, they would need to earn it. Others simply didn't know how to earn it in their families. In some families the requirements for receiving love and approval are too high. In others the requirements are too hard to even figure out. But children always want to be loved. In the abusive family, members get so much negative treatment that they conclude they are never

Love to the human spirit is like water to the body. It is essential.

going to meet the conditions under which love would be granted. Messages of love have to compete with too many messages of disapproval. There exists a feeling of emptiness and loneliness, of being unwanted, unimportant, and of little value. Children who feel this way are sometimes able to develop self-love as adults, but have a hard time doing so because of their confusion as children.

Rate this personal characteristic here._____

Also rate each child in your family here._____ _____

_____ _____ _____

3. An excessive need for control

Some individuals perceive that life and people are hard to control. They thus seek to control everything because they feel that control makes things better and more predictable. They may end up using unhealthy means of obtaining control, like anger or compulsiveness. They are unpredictable and often explosive. Anger may prove to be a powerful control mechanism. When life feels out of control, they can use anger to make things happen the way they want them to. They feel they somehow need to get control of their family environment and make it be more what they want it to be.

They are often afraid of other people's anger. They learn to use anger to combat the anger of others, often attempting to control the situation by getting angry first. They perceive anger *as power to control.* They often report being hypervigilant. They watch everything to make sure nothing goes wrong. They overreact to situations in their life where they perceive things are beginning to go out of control. Sometimes they create a feeling of control by deciding how they want things to be and then not allowing anything to disrupt their plans. Their need for such control is often frustrating to those around them, as they tend to disregard the desires and feelings of others in order to maintain things as they want them to be. To them, control is essential to their well-being.

Rate this personal characteristic here._____

Also rate each child in your family here._____ _____

_____ _____ _____

4. The urge to deny and cover up perceived damage in themselves

Individuals who come from less functional families commonly use artificial covers or "costumes" to prevent others from finding out that they are "damaged goods." The damaged self can be covered with an infinite variety of costumes. Some try to cover their self-perceived damage with success, anger, or humor. Some use physical things, like beautiful clothing, as ornaments to dazzle onlookers. Some cover it up with shyness, and some with emotional distance. The point is they are "hiding out." They want to prevent others from seeing what they don't like in themselves. This is intended to prevent criticism. These individuals do not really know themselves very well. So much energy goes into covering up what they don't like about themselves that real and accurate self-awareness does not develop.

As adults they commonly look for "merit badges" that can give evidence to themselves and others that they are more acceptable than they feel they are. They desperately try to *prove their worth* and *value* to themselves and others. They may use their careers, looks, children, and all kinds of achievements and accomplishments to prove they are something they privately fear they are not. Some may decide to become ultraresponsible. "Give me a job," they say, "and I will *always* do it A+. I will be successful and take care of things. Then you *can't* criticize me. I am the 'responsible, take-care-of-things person of the century.' I am an expert at hiding. I have many covers to protect myself from scrutiny. You can't find the 'real me' to criticize and hurt."

Rate this personal characteristic here._____

Also rate each child in your family here._____ _____

_____ _____ _____

5. Difficulty with intimacy and closeness

Intimacy refers to the interconnection of one life with other lives in a healthy and meaningful way. People from less functional family backgrounds often have major trouble with such intimacy. Why? Because trying to get close to others in the past produced nothing but trouble, heartache, and hurt. True intimacy looks threatening to these individuals. It is a big risk. It requires that they let others know more than just superficial facts about themselves. It requires the sharing of the inner self. In the past, attempts at closeness and self-disclosure have usually resulted in harm and pain.

Many individuals with this problem also report that physical closeness presents a problem. It scares them. In the past, it meant getting hurt and losing trust in someone. Some just don't know how to be close. They have never experienced it and are intimidated by it. It is common that these people, as adults, may be very sexual because to them sex is an act, and it does not necessarily require true intimacy. In turn, their sexual partners feel somewhat unfulfilled by the lack of true closeness that is a necessary part of a healthy sexual relationship. The physical aspect of sex is easy to participate in, whereas true intimacy requires trust, openness, and work in order to build a two-way relationship, something many of these individuals have little experience with. For people who fear intimacy, relationships—and all they require—are too threatening. They are seen as traps that typically slam shut on them, causing severe harm.

Rate this personal characteristic here._____

Also rate each child in your family here._____ _____

_____ _____ _____

6. *Feelings of distrust for others*

People who distrust others are not trusting because they think they'll be disappointed and let down. Distrust is a way of preventing disappointment and hurt. It is a safeguard. It works like a shield and keeps others at a distance. Distance is the key to preventing further hurt. In normal situations trust is earned. But with this type of people it takes significant work to gain trust because *distrust* is *automatic*. Others are rarely able to break through the barrier of distrust.

Rate this personal characteristic here._____

Also rate each child in your family here._____ _____

_____ _____ _____

7. *Feelings of depression*

Individuals get depressed for many reasons, so how is this characteristic unique to people from less functional family backgrounds? One of the unique reasons for depression in the person with a troubled family background is that he or she uses depression as a *hideout*. It is a way of dropping out so that they don't have to deal with the distrust, fear, hurt, anger, and guilt they feel. They just emotionally drop out! It is easier to be depressed. They don't have to think, act, or do anything! They can just emotionally "go away" for a while and not think. It is emotional anesthesia.

There can be a certain amount of self-pity wrapped up in this one as well. People who exhibit this characteristic have been mistreated all their lives, so feeling bad is to be expected. For them, it is easier to hide out with their feelings of depression than face life—past or present. The depressed person may feel like hiding from life works, except that it's very sad in the hideout.

Rate this personal characteristic here._____

Also rate each child in your family here._____ _____

_____ _____ _____

8. Feelings of guilt

Some individuals tend to carry around loads of guilt. Guilt about what? *About themselves, of course!* They think such things as "Maybe if I were a better person, the members of my family, as well as others in general, would love and like me more. Maybe they would love me, care for me, be there for me, protect me, and serve me much more! Since they don't do those things, it must be *me, the unworthy person that I am,* who is to blame for all my trouble!" They often feel unexplainably bad and then feel guilty about feeling bad.

These individuals can be in a situation where they are not responsible for the results but will feel guilty about them anyway! It seems silly to others, but it is real to them. Sometimes they start to feel like there is something they should feel guilty about, they just can't put their fingers on exactly what it is. They *feel bad about being themselves* and about everything else in general. Some even report feeling guilty about feeling guilty!

Rate this personal characteristic here._____

Also rate each child in your family here._____ _____

_____ _____ _____

9. Feelings of low self-esteem

Many people from less functional families feel it is impossible to have a healthy self-image simply because the caretakers in their lives don't value them. The ones who know the most about them, reject them. They continually work hard at trying to get approval from others but never feel that the approval is sufficient or consistent enough. They seek "merit badges," which are evidences of personal success that everyone can see. Personal merit badges take many forms. Looks, accomplishments, awards, ways of impressing others through getting their attention, or any other demonstrable form of success. Sometimes, however, the "merit badge hunt" just becomes too much and these folks give up. They become depressed and angry. They may even report feeling depressed and angry *because* they feel that they are forced to do the merit badge hunt. They really don't like themselves and don't know how to feel otherwise. And even if they achieve many merit badges, underneath it all there is still a mountain of self-doubt.

As a side note, are you noticing how so many of these characteristics are interrelated? Anger, distrust, fear, guilt, and low self-esteem all have a common origin. They are all born of common parentage: experiences in the less functional and thereby troubled family.

Rate this personal characteristic here._____

Also rate each child in your family here._____ _____

_____ _____ _____

10. A feeling that they are different

Growing up in an unusual family, where the dynamics and general health of the family are different from what they seem to be in other families, causes some people to feel they are not like others. They label themselves as "different." "Others seem to be resilient and have more positive attitudes," they say. "Others don't have phobias, depression, anger, self-criticism, fear and anxiety, trouble with intimacy, or guilt." The list of bad traits that others *don't* possess seems endless. These people feel like their "different" home life produced a "different" them. They feel odd. When they join a group, their first feelings are ones of fear that everyone else will discover how different they are.

Rate this personal characteristic here._____

Also rate each child in your family here._____ _____

_____ _____ _____

11. The desire to please

Pleasers are so worried about what people want from them and why people like or dislike them that they believe the only way to be happy is to make sure everyone else is happy. Pleasers have a hard time being honest and sharing their true feelings. Doing so might mean rejection. They don't contradict others. They are "yes-men," agreeing and saying yes to everything, even those things they don't want to do. Their motivation is to prevent others from causing them emotional harm.

In the end, this means that they can't be true to themselves or their real thoughts and feelings on any given subject. As long as everyone else is happy, they are willing to suffer privately. No one will know they are hurting.

They often develop caretaker roles in relation to others. They wear themselves out listening, helping, and doing whatever others want them to do to. They operate under the basic premise that happiness comes from what others think of them. They are extremely dependent on the external judgments of others.

Rate this personal characteristic here._____

Also rate each child in your family here._____ _____

_____ _____ _____

12. Inability to have fun

Some take life too seriously. They believe there is no room for fun. They have to keep busy and may assume the role of high achiever to prove to those around them that they are competent and worthy of attention and approval. They worry that they can't do enough to ensure a great and enduring image in the eyes of others, *so they work harder!* Subsequently, there is no time for fun. At the core, they doubt their own goodness and capabilities and consequently devote all of their time to creating *evidence* that they really are smart and successful and worthy of love and approval. Some are simply too depressed to have fun.

Rate this personal characteristic here._____

Also rate each child in your family here._____ _____

_____ _____ _____

CONCLUSION

By reviewing these characteristics and rating yourself and your children according to their descriptions, you may have identified some new areas to work on. You may now better understand the family you came from and how it affected you. You may understand how you have reacted to whatever went on in your family of origin and how your children are reacting to their family of origin. Again, *all* families have some difficulty in these areas. Dysfunction is not an either/or, meaning it either exists or doesn't exist in your family. Every family has some form of dysfunction. Some may find very little evidence of trouble in their family of origin or in the family they are now raising, while others will find more things that need attention. I am not trying to make you focus exclusively on the negative, but am looking for ways to help you foster growth and development in your own family. One step in that process is to identify important areas that need work.

Many individuals feel compelled to work at building healthier families because they already see in themselves the effects of the less functional families they came from. Perhaps, as you read through this chapter and did the self-evaluation, you learned something about your family of origin and about who you are today. That will influence how you parent. It will influence the role you play in your current family. Without some degree of self-understanding, you are like a rudderless ship trying to make its way to an important destination.

Remember, you don't have to be perfectly healthy to work at being a good parent. Many quite imperfect people do some wonderful things as parents.

Perhaps what you have learned here will help you to identify the path you need to travel to be a healthier person, and thus a healthier parent or family member. Remember, you don't have to be perfectly healthy to work at being a good parent. Many quite imperfect people do some wonderful things as parents. Often, their imperfections make them more approachable to their children. Their imperfections can also help parents understand the imperfections of others, including their children. These imperfections can be quite humbling and may make better people and better parents out of them.

Some of you have traveled a very difficult and demanding course as you have experienced the pains of family life. But maybe it has taught you something. Perhaps it has left you somewhat inspired regarding what you want to do with your family right now. I hope it has not left you too deflated. Not long ago someone asked me how I got free of my troubled past. First I told them that no one gets *entirely* free of their past, even if they want to. But, at a certain point in my early adult life, I did make a crucial decision. In terms of healthy living, I had lost much of my past, but I was not going to also lose my future if I could have a say in it.

Learn from the past, but don't let it determine your future. As Thomas Paine once said, "The harder the conflict, the more glorious the triumph. What we obtain too cheaply, we esteem too lightly" (*The Crisis,* no. 1). Some of our best lessons are those hardest learned. Wisdom does not carry a cheap price tag.

It certainly helps to confront areas of weakness and to work to strengthen them. Now, there is one necessity if you want to get on track to be the kind of parent you want to be: You must understand what goes into the making of a healthy family. Once you understand that, then you can go after it.

You can do it step by step and little by little. You can get better at it *over time.* I am sure of that. I know some of you are too hard on yourselves as parents. And some of you need to be harder on yourselves in some areas and wake up to the reality of what your family needs you to be. I wish I could somehow know which of you reading this book needs more *compassion* from me and who needs a *stiff challenge.* You will have to decide which you need. But with the understanding gained from looking into less functional families, let's now begin to talk about the specific characteristics of a more functional family.

CHAPTER 4

Leadership

I enjoy watching a particular family that lives just down the street from me. I regularly see this family taking walks together—Mom, Dad, and children. I see the parents at the ballpark as they watch their children participate in games. Quite often a number of the other children come to watch a brother or sister. They yell to them in support and cheer them on. I see them walking to church together. Once a week I see them having Family Evening together in their living room. They talk, play, and eat goodies together. I think they like each other. They are not well-known. But the parents don't seem to care. What they really seem to care about is where the family is going and what each family member can become. The children have caught the spirit of their parents' efforts. This family is certainly not without problems, though the parents have seemed capable in handling their problems. I have talked to them in their front yard before and know that they have the same concerns I have as they try to run their family. All of this makes me like the "feel" of their family. I like that the parents are noticeably committed to the family's well-being. They are intentionally and actively parenting their children. They have what I like to call *a committed-family attitude.*

In the many years that I have observed, talked to, and interacted with families, I have stumbled onto a characteristic that embodies the type of leadership present in the family just described. It is actually very simple, but it caught me off guard and surprised me a bit when I first noticed it. One day, after interviewing a family very similar to my neighbors down the street, it hit me that these parents are focused and confident. But focused and confident in what? That they can achieve anything and everything they want to in their family? No. Confident of positive outcomes? No, but they have confidence in their sense of family dedication and direction. They know how much they care about their family, and they have decided to put a lot of effort into it. Their family is their chief life focus. They make many choices each week to give time and attention to their family rather than to something else more exciting or less complicated. They understand that they will sometimes have to sacrifice if their family is to get what it needs. They don't resent what they may need to give—or give up—to be good parents and leaders.

A Shared Family Vision

The parents I describe have helped to develop a *shared vision* of what the family is all about and where it is going together. These parents exhibit *focused and confident leadership* in their family. You can sense it as you talk to them. A sense of dedication is in the air. There is, inherent in the family vision communicated by the parents to family members, a certainty, a confidence, and a clear path to follow as a family. That path feels good to members of the family. Children trust their parents because of the consistency they feel and the confidence they see. The parents' focused and committed leadership affects the entire family atmosphere. The parents know they are models for the rest of the family. They carefully and consciously choose what they model. They actually talk about themselves as family models. They know they are fighting a daily battle for the well-being of their children. They know they need to be well prepared.

Inherent in the family vision communicated by parents to family members should be a certainty, a confidence, and a clear path to follow as a family.

It is also obvious that they don't fulfill their roles perfectly. They know they do not need to. In the face of challenges, they recognize their leadership responsibilities and step to the front, letting the family know that they will try to do their best to maintain committed family relationships. When they doubt or feel insecure, they have each other. Together they can strengthen feeble knees and walk arm in arm, supporting each other. How they feel about each other and their dedication to their family is a fixed conviction and an established value.

Now, it is clear that not everyone can embrace feelings like those just described on exactly the same level; but if parents openly desire and seek after such attitudes, they send out a call to their children about their shared family vision. Because the parents know where they are trying to go, the family has much more confidence in where it is going.

YOU CAN COUNT ON US

This type of parental leadership can make all the difference in a family. Why? Because parents who think and act like leaders with a shared family vision are able to say to their children, "You can count on us." And, at the core, that is what children want: to be able to count on their parents. What are they counting on? Perfect parenting? No. They don't need perfect parents, but they do need committed parents. How are you leading your family? Can your children count on you? Do a quick ten-scale evaluation, and then discuss the results in Family Discussion Time.

Key Characteristics of Great Parent-Leaders

The parents in these families seem to have a very reasonable and down-to-earth perception of things. They avoid trying to "make things happen" by way of negative emotions, such as anger. They work to decrease contention in the home. These parent-leaders do not manage coercively. Rather, they possess a unique type of much calmer *internal strength* that helps them do their work as leaders of a family. This parental strength feels stable and firm.

At the core, children want to be able to count on their parents.

I have a hunch about the makeup of their internal strength. I suggest that these parents share four significant characteristics. Please do a ten-scale evaluation of yourself on these characteristics in your family project notebook.

1. Humility _____

2. Integrity _____

3. A desire to serve others _____

4. Possession of a clear personal purpose and mission within the family _____

These four traits create people who are sufficiently selfless and have personal values that are consistently reflected in their behavior. They are more able to look outside themselves as they consider the needs of others and serve within the family. And they know what their responsibilities and personal purposes are within their family. These four characteristics—I like to call them the internal mix—constitute the heart of a parent who can assertively exhibit leadership within the more func-

Healthy parents avoid trying to "make things happen" by way of negative emotions.

tional family. Please remember that I have described them quite ideally. The ideal is good to know because it gives us something to shoot for. Of course, none of us is all the way there right now. As you look to the ideal, let's consider what else helps parents to be good leaders in the home.

THEY KNOW THEY WON'T GET EVERYTHING THEY WANT

Good parent-leaders do not let the family casually float through life. Their hands are on the helm in an obvious way. But in their hopes, dreams, and plans for their family, capable parents have a certain amount of common sense and an ability to understand that they will not get everything they want from their parenting efforts. They know that, and they are okay with it. They still move ahead and keep working.

They know they are trying to give their family their "best shot" and that is the most important thing they can do. They also know that the one thing they can always give is hard work and faithful effort. They also know that final outcomes take years to develop, and that it takes a lot of patience to wait for the fruits of their labors in the family. Today's investment in the family may not produce dividends until many years later. Wise parents have learned patience. They are poignantly aware that sometimes parents are called upon to give much without seeing the results they desire. That is part of faithful parenting. After all, you are a parent because you accepted the responsibility to be one, not because it will always produce what you hoped for. To parent in the face of supreme disappointment demonstrates that you have great character and are someone to be admired and respected. Take a moment to rate yourself on the ten-scale in this area.

I know I won't get everything I want as a parent, and that's okay!_____

Some of you may be discouraged in this area simply because it's so hard to feel focused and confident in today's competitive world. There are a lot of messages out there—and all of them say something different about how you should parent and what's important. We've all felt confused and overwhelmed. In fact, there is no simple, magical answer that will resolve this type of parental confusion. However, I do have many practical suggestions about what you can do to improve things in your family.

In their hopes, dreams, and plans for their family, capable parents have a certain amount of common sense and an ability to understand that they will not get everything they want from their parenting efforts.

Here's one now: Decide that you will offer a fairly well-thought-out plan for your family and then step back to allow the results to be whatever they will be. This will help you as a parent not to feel so responsible for making everything turn out just right.

Here's another one: Parenting is a big sacrifice that does not carry with it guaranteed results. But it does carry with it a guaranteed opportunity to offer what you can in loving service to your family. Seek an A grade in "trying" rather than in producing certain results.

THEY ARE PASSIONATE ABOUT THEIR ROLES

A parental *passion* for family usually leads to a significant investment in the family. This is so important. The passion a parent feels toward the family leads to a greater-than-average investment in the family. Passionate parents are willing to give up other things to attend to family needs. Even in the face of catastrophic family problems, these parents maintain their devotion to their fundamental family role and responsibility. They attempt to face their family burdens with dignity and devotion.

Where does that passion come from? It comes from an interesting type of self-confidence, one that is not at all arrogant. Parents with this type of passion are acutely aware that the job of parenting is much bigger than they are. In a fascinating way, they are clearly connected to something else. *They have faith in something greater.* What is it? For some it is religious faith, but it is always faith in their *own* vision of the purpose of *their* family. This helps them be passionate about their families. They can verbalize what their vision of their family is all about. And so they regularly talk about it with their children. Their children often become passionate about it as well.

The word *vision* keeps coming back to me when I think of great parent-leaders. Their vision is such that it affects their daily decisions, and they realize that each of their personal decisions affects the family. They view decisions from the family perspective. I recall years ago hearing a story about Ezra Taft Benson, who was Secretary of Agriculture in the Cabinet of President Dwight D. Eisenhower. Mr. Benson made it clear that he would not attend meetings or functions on a particular night of the week so that he could be home with his family that night. It was the night they had set aside to have regular family time together. I remember thinking, "If he can do it, so can I." In that aspect of family life, Mr. Benson and his family knew what they were about. It must have been part of their family vision. This whole idea of "knowing what you are about" in the family is a topic you can go over and over in Family Discussion Time. Take a moment and rate yourself on the ten-scale in this area.

I am passionate about being a parent._____

My passion helps direct the way I parent._____

THEY HAVE PERSONAL INTEGRITY

Many of the best parent-leaders I have interviewed possess noticeable *personal integrity*. Their personal and public lives seem to integrate fairly well. I have even asked some of their older children about this integrity, and they generally agree that this integrity is in the forefront of their parents' lives. The children see that their parents have integrated personal and public lives. But they are not perfect people, nor is that a big concern to them. They try hard to be strong, solid leaders in their family, but they are quite aware of their own inadequacies. They seem to be okay with the fact that they are fairly average people in many ways. That is hopeful: Average people can make good parents if they figure out together what they are trying to do in the family. I have a feeling that these parents are good role models for children. Why? Because what they espouse—based upon their clearly communicated values—and what they subsequently do match quite closely. The world needs many more people like that. Rate yourself in this area.

My personal integrity is evident in both my personal and my public life._____

THEY ARE OPEN

I have also noticed a type of healthy *openness* in the parent-leaders I observe. They can be scrutinized. They receive feedback.

They do not need to protect themselves too much. They know how important their example is, and they want that example to be a good one. They try to be open to evaluation—their own (in Family Discussion Time) as well as that from other sources. They can even be scrutinized, to a certain degree, by their children. Not scrutinized in a rude or disrespectful way, but open to feedback children sometimes give. They seek to be less defensive. This is another characteristic on my certain-to-become-famous ten-scale. I've found that the most healthy parents score well in this area; they get a 6 or a 7 and sometimes even higher. Rate yourself on this characteristic.

I am open to evaluation and feedback._____

THEY DO NOT COMPETE WITH OTHER FAMILIES

Part of great parental leadership is the ability to remove yourself and your family from the competitive arena that encompasses so much of daily life. Good parent-leaders know what they and their family are about and focus on the internal performance of their own family. The comparisons they make are to the ideal family they want to become. They might collect good ideas from other families to use as they improve their own. But this is always done with a sense that perfection is not the goal. They just want to be good enough in comparison with their own ideal. And their ideal is of their own making.

Good parent-leaders know what they and their family are about and focus on the internal performance of their own family.

I know how hard it is to not make life a competition between yourself and the "perfect person." I wish we could do better at accepting our own imperfections—and those of our children. I encourage families to talk about competition and help their children learn that *life is a project* and that you can be happily imperfect while headed in the right direction. If parents can talk openly and hopefully about the topic of personal imperfection, then they can help each other. If you want to experience progress, then you must be able to talk about the need for improvement. You must recognize that your family is not like anyone else's, and it doesn't need to be.

THEY HAVE A VISION

Here it is again: Parent-leaders are more effective if they have a family vision. Do *you* have a vision of why *you* are a family? Does that vision give your family future direction? Does it energize you and give you motivation to work hard for your family? Does it help you know what to put your energy into in day-to-day family life? I believe that the concept of *the family vision* works best if it is kept simple. It represents what you care about with all the combined hearts in your family. And anyone over the age of eight or ten should be able to fully understand it. The vision Sherri and I have of our family is represented by the following (not listed in order of priority):

Teach your children that life is a project and that you can be happily imperfect while headed in the right direction.

The MacArthur Family

We are together as a family to—
- Help all family members feel important, significant, and competent
- Love, honor, and respect one another
- Help each other love learning and seek education
- Learn to care for others and give service
- Have lots of fun together
- Worship and serve God together

In other words, those six things are the MacArthur *family values*. They represent what we care about in our family.

You might find it interesting to do a quick ten-scale evaluation of how you think you are currently doing on your own family values. What are your family values? What is your family vision? How would you state it in a few sentences? If you don't have one, just create one as a working piece that you can discuss and work on in Family Discussion Time.

A family vision is a great thing to work for. *It really is why you are together.* Think and talk about these things over and over in Family Discussion Time and in Family Council when all the family is together. You could take one item from your family vision and just talk about it and share experiences. Put your family values up in some obvious place in your home. They will serve as a good visual reminder of your family values and commitments. It is motivating to do things like that. All this helps your family to know what is the center of your family life and what you care about most. If someone asked your children what you, as parents, care about the most, could your children answer the question? What *must* you absolutely pass on to your children? Do a ten-scale evaluation in this category.

My family has a shared vision._____

My children know what that vision is._____

THEY ARE FLEXIBLE IN THEIR LEADERSHIP PRACTICES

Great parent-leaders are flexible leaders. They understand that children want clear, focused, and flexible leadership from parents. Children want to respect you without fearing you. They want you to lead them, guide them, but not *drive* them.

I used to run a youth treatment program for troubled adolescents. It was interesting to see how many of the parents knew of only two ways to do things: the right way (their way) and the wrong way (any other way). Parents must not be too rigid in their approach to children; being a "black-or-white thinker" can lead to much difficulty when parenting. Parents must be fair-minded and learn to see that there are many different—and valid—points of view regarding family life and family feelings.

Children want clear, focused, and flexible leadership from parents. Children want to respect you without fearing you. They want you to lead them, guide them, but not drive them.

Parents who are willing to sit down with their children and generate many possible solutions to a particular problem can often come out with better solutions. Learning to understand and deal with perspectives different from their own is an important way in which children grow into mature adults. One way to help them with such development is to ask for their opinions on various things that come up in the family. One of the great parental building phrases of family life is "What do you think about . . . ?" Another is "What is your opinion on . . . ?" This is a great Family Council activity when working on a problem or plan together. What are you saying to your child when you ask for her opinion? You are saying, "You are competent; that is why I want your opinion" or "You are important to our family and that is why I want your opinion." Doing so helps build children into healthy adults who are able to work with points of view that are different from their own.

Dialogue like the following occurs in many homes:

A child says, "I want to go to my friend's house to do my homework."

The parent thinks, "Wrong. In our family we do homework at home. That is why it is called *home*work!" The parent says, while thinking he or she is right, "I told you that I don't want you over there at that time of day. End of discussion."

Although this is a very common scenario, it's also very rigid and doesn't send a message that this parent is flexible and open-minded.

Even as you read that example, you may have thought something like this: "The parents probably have a good reason for saying that and, after all, they are the parents and they know better." True, but that is not the point. The point here is that children generally do not respond well to rigidity and inflexibility in a parent's thinking. They respond better in a situation where the child's view is discussed and respected. Parents should discuss and respect the child's view often enough that their children learn to think and respect their own opinions, even if they are not as mature. Parents are the gardeners and are "growing" children into adults.

The approach that "You will not be permitted to think in our home; you can do that *after* you leave" is a dangerous one. I want my children to try out their thinking while they are with me, so that I can hear what they have to say and help them. If I do not encourage them to think, then I will not be aware of the kind of thinking they are doing. I may then be surprised at how they think after they leave my home.

I *especially* want to know my children's opinions on things that are of the greatest importance to me. If they are at variance with me in one of those areas, I really want to know it. That is when I encourage the most talking and do the most listening, especially if I suspect trouble. If the general parental approach is that you *order* and don't *discuss,* your children will stop thinking, and then what will they do when they are on their own and have to think for themselves? Children who are given sufficient opportunity to think for themselves tend to develop greater self-respect.

Both children and parents must seek to understand each other. How they *both* think about things should be fairly considered. The conclusion reached may be different than what either considered at the beginning, but both parties will feel more understood and hopefully happier with the conclusion. You have to trust yourself and your child if this is to occur. Some of the great shocks of my life have come at Family Councils that included older children and I've found that their insights and wisdom have exceeded my own. Now that they are older I regularly ask for their opinions and help in personal and family matters.

Children who are given sufficient opportunity to think for themselves tend to develop greater self-respect.

Take some time to evaluate yourself in this area.

I am not rigid in my parenting style._____

I respect and ask for my children's opinions on appropriate subjects._____

THEY PRACTICE FAIR-MINDED AND COURTEOUS LEADERSHIP

I like to call what I described above *fair-minded leadership.* It means children can be heard and their points of view can be considered. It does not mean the parents are weak and give up power. It means they respect the children and can be fair-minded in their approach to the situation at hand.

Under this model, parents invite their children's input, thoughts, and recommendations. You raise your children's self-esteem by communicating that you believe they can think, reason, and help determine an appropriate conclusion to the matter. What if they can't? Then show them how to do it, and help them try again. Fair-minded leadership is most successful if it is done with *parental courtesy.*

In some problem-solving situations, using a Family Council can teach everyone to respect each other, hear each other, and learn to solve problems together. Children learn how to do these things by watching you take the lead and show them the way. If you fear giving them a chance to think and communicate with you because they will fight with you, then use Family Councils to teach them how to communicate differently. Children will learn they are part of a family team. At the conclusion of such a council, tell the children what you did and why you did it, so they see the family principle of respectfully working together in action.

You raise your children's self-esteem by communicating that you believe they can think, reason, and help determine an appropriate conclusion to the matter.

If you are fearful to attempt family teaching because you lack experience, don't give up. Practice. Talk over how you want to approach it in Family Discussion Time so you go into it as well prepared as you can. Your children will see you trying and learning as you go. That is good. Family leadership is an ongoing learning experience for parents. Don't be afraid to start out by saying, "I am a little nervous about this. I hope you will help me. I think it is important for us to start learning some things together."

THE REST OF US!

Now, let me speak to those of you who are reading this, thinking the preceding characteristics are unattainable. Maybe you're asking something like this: "And what if I don't have enough personal integrity?" or this: "What if I am not clear on where I am leading my family?" or "What if I have few leadership skills?"

Welcome to the "Millions of Us Who Feel That Way" club!

Let the ten-scale evaluations lead you there. If you find you are at 4 when it comes to establishing a clear direction for your family, then talk together about how to move ahead to a 6. This is a great Family Discussion Time topic. What you do to move from 4 to 6 will make all the difference. Your children will likely notice you are trying and working at this. Children learn how to run families by watching their parents. What are they learning from you?

Here's an example of what a child can learn from a parent: I worked with a university student advisor for a number of years who had developed a professional image as a highly capable person. After marrying and adopting a little boy, she announced she was leaving the university so that she could be more available to teach and spend time with her young son. If she could have worked a few years longer, she would have had a good retirement. She gave that up. I remember how impressed I was by the sacrifice she made. She was trying to demonstrate a greater commitment to her family. I hope her little boy appreciates what his mother did when he gets older. I'll remind him!

Perhaps your concern for your family will encourage you to do some talking with other parents about how they view their families and their commitment to them. Motivation is often contagious. Motivation can help you move up on the ten-scale. And remember that you don't need to suddenly be at an 8 on the ten-scale. A 3 probably won't be good enough for you or your family. But if you could tackle the challenge of shooting for 5, you and your children would notice some big differences in the family.

Another thing that has helped me is to project my current attitudes into the future. In other words, I ask myself, "If I remain as I am, and continue to consider my family as I do, what will happen?" I also ask, "What will happen if I make some changes?" Often such conversations with yourself are very helpful. *Someday the future will be now.* What will it be like for your family? Just keep working at it. And stay open-minded. Use the ten-scale to rate your general ability as a parent-leader. Then talk about it at Family Discussion Time and make improvements if you feel they are needed.

I am committed to being a parent-leader._____

I am focused and confident in my role as a leader._____

I remember the story of Benjamin Franklin and his core values and morals. He had thirteen values he had identified to live by. He was so serious about it that he would work his way through them, attempting to improve and build them more completely into his life, and then start over again at the first one, working his way through them all over again! (*Autobiography of Benjamin Franklin.*)

Focused and confident leaders in the family know they are always *in process.* Actually, everything about developing families is regularly in process. That is one of the fundamental concepts of healthy family life. We *know* we are not *"there."* But we care about working hard at getting *"more there."*

CHAPTER 5

Can I Guarantee How My Children Turn Out?

Results. They are something that many people pay a lot of attention to, particularly in Western culture. And is there any place where we care more about how things turn out than in our families? But can I guarantee how my children will turn out if I work hard enough at my parenting and completely dedicate myself it to it? I want my children to turn out great. I bet you want yours to turn out great too.

I've thought about this a lot and, over time, I have determined that I really can't control how my children turn out. I can, however, be totally sure that I put my best efforts into raising my children as well as I can. This is what I have tried—and continue to try—to do. Part of my parenting effort is to get really clear on the goals I want to help each of my children achieve. But then what? I move my emphasis to what I am going to do to help them get to their goals.

I am *not* saying results don't matter. They do, but we must be careful not to make them matter too much. Getting results can bear undue influence on how we behave as parents. Many parents want to *make* their families be a certain way. Their objective is to get the job done and done well. They are looking for evidence that will verify their parenting efforts are paying off; they want A's on the parenting report card, and they believe that A's are based on how their children turn out.

YOU CAN'T COMPLETELY CONTROL OUTCOMES

In the more functional family, parents realize that they simply can't get *too* caught up in results. They care about results, but they know that what they offer their children—regardless of how it is received or what it produces—should be the main focus. As a parent, what you offer your children is within your control; what they do with it is not.

Parents who are too results oriented may contribute to negative fallout in family relationships or even reduce the general well-being of family members. With results as the ultimate parental objective, the price for success can often be too high. Don't fall for the old, ends-justify-the-means argument. The family is not a business where outcomes regularly make or break the organization and its purposes. The family has a unique purpose in *continuing* to work with its members, even in moments of failure or disappointment.

What you offer your children is within your control; what they do with it is not.

Let's go back to something more basic as we think about why we parent in the first place. Would you be willing to consider that being a parent in the family is, to a certain degree, its own reward? At least on a good day? This is an honor that goes beyond even the idea of a duty. Of course, we all hope for happy outcomes in the family. The hard work we do is sometimes tough to endure if we do not see good results. But there has to be something deeper and more fundamental at the heart of our parenting efforts, even if outcomes are not always quickly forthcoming. *You are a child's life guide and mentor.* As she tries to figure out how to live life, she has you. If she struggles in trying to do that well, she still has you. What a privilege to play that role in her life. Your staying power as a parent is essential. Mike Ditka, former coach of the Chicago Bears, once said, "The ability to stay in the game is what counts."

It is crucial that you view your parental role as important not only when things go well in the family, but always. You are the coach of a team. Does it make sense to value and honor that role only when the team is winning and all players are healthy? Keep coaching even when players struggle and the team has ups and downs. Firmly believing in this idea can save parents from giving up when they go through periods of major struggle with children. What coach would walk off the field and quit when, despite his best efforts, his players have been pushed back to their own five-yard line? He might want to, but he doesn't. He may be glad for a break in the action at half-time, but he knows he will return to the field. Coaches who don't leave the stadium when their team is losing—and parents who don't give up when their family is struggling—are an inspiration to their players.

The reason focusing too much on outcomes can be problematic is that results are not guaranteed, no matter how hard you work at achieving them. Sometimes you may get the results you want but later find they are accompanied by negative attitudes and hurt feelings. You may get a star power forward, but he could be an angry power forward. You may "produce" a straight-A student, but she could be a depressed and anxious valedictorian. You may get a child who always does the right thing but end up with a shaky relationship with that child because of what you did to produce the successful outcome. You may get a child who seems to be right on the money with everything but on the inside is fragile and insecure, fearful of making a mistake.

Sometimes the outcomes become too important. When you really look at yourself and your parenting styles and motivations, do you ever find that part of your hard work and effort to produce a successful family is to make you look good? We all hope our children will make us look good, but be careful that that particular motive does not carry too much weight in your overall parenting equation.Whatever your motives are, be careful not to legitimize using pressure and intimidation to make a child behave a certain way. Doing so has a tendency to damage relationships over time and to produce undesirable outcomes.

Sometimes you really might not understand your motives. Life can be very complicated, and it's often hard to determine why you behave in one way or another. You might want to check your motives every now and then by asking yourself why you work so hard for particular outcomes in your family. Ask yourself if you ever force outcomes. It's one thing to force an outcome for the well-being of your child; it's another thing to force an outcome simply because you feel the need to be viewed by others as a successful parent. You can live much more peacefully as a parent if you focus on what you can offer your children rather than on what they do with what you have offered them. It will also produce a healthier, more relaxed, and less-stressed environment for your children as well.

CHILDREN AS MERIT BADGES

Just like children, parents need a healthy sense of worth and self-esteem to make it through life. Where do you find your self-esteem? I have found that the happiest parents base theirs on things over which they have adequate control. Among the least happy parents are those who base their self-esteem on the success of their children. In a sense, their children have become like merit badges. All of us probably do a little of

Whatever your motives are, be careful not to legitimize using pressure and intimidation to make a child behave a certain way.

this to some extent—our children are great lots of times and can really make us proud. Trouble comes when parents try to "script" the family, forgetting that children are children and sometimes have different hopes and expectations than do the parents. Parents can get caught up in following an intangible script that says they must produce successful children who always do the right things. This type of parenting often involves pressure tactics designed to achieve certain results. This can be very dangerous and may backfire on parents. The pressure to turn out right may get so tough that children turn against the very things their parents want so much. I once heard a story of a young man whose parents described at his Eagle Scout Court of Honor how they had kept his "nose to the grindstone" to ensure he became an Eagle Scout. When it was the son's turn to say some final remarks, he simply said, "I hope they are happy," and sat down.

Most of us have good motives. Not every parent who tries to push a child to success is motivated by selfish reasons. Generally, parents want the best for their children. But to be completely honest, parents may need to consider how their own needs become a part of what they want for their children. *How much do you need your children to make you look good?* I am certain that all parents hope their children make them look good! I certainly do. But when that becomes *the* driving force in parenting, there can be a problem. Focusing too much on results brings tense and unhappy feelings into the home. Watch out for those types of feelings in your home. They can ruin the family atmosphere and are clear danger signals that too much parental pressure is being applied.

If there is anything I want you to remember from this chapter, it is this: Don't be obsessed with results. Parents who have an agenda are often threatening and ominous to their children. Parent-child relationships become difficult to maintain in such an atmosphere because the child's success is a product that must be produced. Much-needed relationships get lost in the process of creating successful children who don't disappoint their parents.

EXPECTATIONS

During the thirty years that I have been a college professor, I have had my students write a major paper each semester on how they became the people they are today. I have read thousands of papers that have given me a glimpse into a student's life and how that life develops within the context of a family. Numerous times I have read words like this: "I felt my parents were always watching me. I had to perform at very high levels. I felt a lot of pressure not to disappoint them or make them look bad by failing to succeed. It wore me out quite often." Some of that pressure is a natural consequence of appropriate expectations; but another part of it represents the stress many students were under to respond to their parents' needs.

Mild and properly communicated expectations can motivate and guide children. Desperate attempts to make children meet parental expectations can result in too much pressure and a feeling of hostility. That can actually push children into making bad decisions and acting inappropriately. Parents may then forget the more important matter, which is the type of relationship they have with a given child. They may end up communicating that the result is more important than the person.

Don't let your personal expectations get in the way of your relationship with your children. Even more important, don't let your expectations dictate who your children become. A great Family Council topic is "expectations" and how we deal with them in our family. Make it a family topic rather than just a parental topic. Work on expectations together.

The issue of autonomy for each child is vital. As children grow, parents have a responsibility to transfer personal ownership of self to the child, doing so more and more over time. Each child must eventually become his or her own person. That is really what you want, especially if you don't want to be tying shoes and setting up curfews for the rest of your life! For the child to become a mature adult, parents must gradually turn over more and more decision making to the child so that he learns to take care of his own personal life. This happens gradually, based on the age and capability of the child. You do something invaluable when you help your children feel personal satisfaction in their own efforts to become whatever they want to become.

Some parents, however, have a difficult time with this and seek to retain ownership and control of the child for too long. Consequently, the child's personal autonomy and growth suffer. It's almost as if the parent is saying, "I can't allow you to fail, so I'll continue to do and decide for you." How sad for both the parent and the child! As a side note, this can also occur because of insufficient trust in the mind of the parent. Sometimes a lack of trust exists for very good reasons. Trust must be earned. But the parent must also be willing to take the risk of letting go at some point if the child is to learn to be self-managing.

ATTITUDES ABOUT MISTAKES

As you encourage your children to develop a sense of personal self, continue to teach correct principles. Work hard to teach them all you can and then allow them to govern themselves, hoping and praying that things will turn out well. When the process isn't forced, life is simply easier on everyone.

Now comes the big worry: "But what if my children make mistakes?" Here's my response: "Don't we all make mistakes?"

You must trust your children to overcome, learn from, and survive their mistakes. Evaluate your fundamental beliefs about mistakes and errors. They can deepen character and challenge an individual, and they can become the building blocks of growth. Great things can happen when parents teach their children that falling down provides an opportunity to get up again and thereby learn and grow. Falling down carries with it a certain amount of personal sadness and difficulty, but getting up demonstrates that you are doing what you can to regain control of your life and your own well-being. It's a powerful belief. Of course, it's possible to fall down and seem not to get up, but I believe most of us can survive our falls and mistakes. That is where the family comes in. We help get each other up and going again.

You must trust your children to overcome, learn from, and survive their mistakes.

I know a one-year-old who tumbles a lot these days. She's learning to walk, and that's a difficult task. When she first started out, she would fall down and start to cry—probably because she was more startled than hurt. But her wise mom knew what to do. She had observed that this child loved watching her older sisters play softball. So, when the toddler tumbles, her mom yells, "Safe," and moves her arms like an umpire does. The toddler thinks this is hilarious. She has stopped getting upset when she falls. She wants to keep learning this walking thing and knows that whether she falls or not, she'll always be safe. Her mom makes sure of that.

Your children will fall down. Mistakes and errors *will* occur, but everyone in a family can learn from them by helping each other. We fall down *together* and we get up *together* in a family.

WHAT YOU OFFER YOUR CHILDREN IS MOST IMPORTANT

By now you have probably figured out that I believe one of the major points of focus as a parent should be to devote attention to how and what you *offer* your children. This is safer for you and easier for your children. Take some time to think about what you can offer your child to help her achieve her goals and become the kind of person you want her to be *and she wants to be.* Then leave the outcome to her. Somewhere between how you raise her and how she ultimately turns out is her choice.

For example, many parents value good academic habits and performance, hoping their children will value them as well. A parent who is *results oriented* focuses on his child's grade-point average (GPA) or some other concrete fact (like a scholarship) that gives evidence of the child's success. The parent obtains the report card the minute it is printed so he can see if *his* child got the GPA *he* needs him to have. And if the GPA proves inadequate, the parent begins a process of communicating certain expectations to the child, along with the consequences that *will* follow if the child does not meet them. The parent puts on pressure and increases the negative consequences if that GPA or scholarship doesn't happen.

What would a parent who is focused on what to *offer* a child—in the form of help and encouragement—do differently from what the parent does who is focused more exclusively on results? This parent might sit down with her daughter and talk together about the importance of doing well in school, what it requires of her, and the effort and work that goes into it. This parent might offer time and interest to help her child with studying, homework, or practicing. She will provide her child with a good example by being a student herself, acting on her own love of learning. She won't hover over her child and watch her every step. This parent will explain and support, and then she will trust. This parent will tell her child that she is available if the child needs help. This parent will offer all the support and help she can, and then she will trust that the child will accomplish her academic goals herself. There is nothing wrong with rewards occasionally, but this parent focuses on the things mentioned above. Then, when her daughter achieves success, the child has the satisfaction of knowing she did it mostly herself, rather than having her parent engineer the outcome. The parent can be proud of her, and she can be proud of herself.

What if a child doesn't respond to this type of encouragement? In this case, a parent can continue to help and offer encouragement and leave the ball in the child's court. This is where a parent should step back and let the child go for it herself so she can feel the satisfaction of personal success if sufficient success occurs. If you do this, you may have to wrestle with your own need to engineer the outcome and make it happen the way you want it to. You will have to learn how to be satisfied with *offering* help and love to your child. It requires that you have trust in your child rather than forcing the outcome.

A friend once told me about his son who had a somewhat troubled teenage life. The dad was really worried about him and how to help him do better in life. He sought my advice on the matter and asked me what he should do. I told him that it appeared that his son needed a good success experience so that he could start developing some self-confidence. We concluded that the dad would help his son get a job so that the son could begin developing knowledge and skills that would be helpful in his adult life. The dad's "offering" was to go on a job search among people that he knew. The dad was able to find a place where his son could work and develop some worthwhile skills. When we next talked, the dad told me he was worried about turning over the reins of this new experience to his son for fear that he would not do well in it. In addition, it was a friend who had offered the job. He knew he would be embarrassed if his son did not do well.

I encouraged the dad to sit down with his son and have a good talk about the opportunity and what it would require of him. After that he would need to trust his son and leave the rest of the experience up to him. I remember the dad saying, "but he might fail." I acknowledged that this was entirely possible. I also acknowledged that as his son made his way through this new experience, with his dad occasionally checking on how he was doing and offering help, he would have the opportunity to learn many new things and also develop some self-confidence, too. His son would potentially have his own personal success experience. If, at the end, the job worked out in a satisfactory way, this dad could say to his son, "You did it, not me. Congratulations." I also indicated that the outcome might not match the hoped-for expectation. The dad had to wrestle with whether he was going to hover over his son and "make sure" he succeeded or take a risk and let this be his son's experience, for good or for ill.

Interestingly, the boy did not show up on the first day of the new job! The employer called the boy and asked him to come over to his office for a visit. The boy went, and the employer could see that the boy felt very inadequate and frightened at trying a new job. He encouraged the boy to give it a try anyway. The boy agreed (a little encouragement goes a long way), and over a period of time he did better and better. The employer told the boy, "You tried, and you did it." The boy's father, who largely stayed out of the situation, was very grateful. He hadn't forced; he had offered. He continued to give offerings by sitting down with his son and giving him encouragement and credit for working hard. This situation might have resulted in failure, but it didn't.

THE FAMILY ALTAR

Much of parenting involves wrestling with emotions like those of the father in the previous story. Offering something of substance to your children is not always easy. It often involves sacrifice—sacrifice of time, personal feelings, pride, and sometimes even money. Because parenting involves sacrifice, I often have parents look at their offerings as such, even going as far as imagining that all they give to their children they offer on a symbolic *altar.*

Suppose one of your children is struggling with some things related to his schooling. Rather than placing emphasis on producing a certain outcome in that part of his life, imagine stepping up to a symbolic altar and placing on it whatever offering or gift you have to give that might be helpful to him. Maybe you could give advice. Or you could provide tutoring or some type of academic help. Maybe you could offer love and support. Possibly you could provide encouragement or a good example. You might even pay his tuition, despite the financial sacrifice for you. Your offering or gift could be many things. The point is that you offer him whatever you can to help him progress in school. Then, once you offer your help and assistance, you *step away* from the altar and let him decide whether or not he accepts the gift that you left there for him to take. It is his decision. He must decide. He must come to the altar and take the gift you left for him. Don't stand by the altar and insist that he take your offering.

The true benefit to him is that every step of the way he is following his *own* goal and walking toward his own achievement; your goals as the parent are secondary. Because determining the outcome is his ultimately his decision to make, he gains the greatest benefit from the resolution. He develops self-confidence and self-esteem because he did it himself. Fundamentally, he feels that what he is working on is *his* project, not yours. Your job is to stand back, applaud, and cheer for him.

Of course, there is always the possibility that he will not come to the altar to take your gift. Or he may come to the altar, pick up the gift, and subsequently throw it down. What you must learn to do is focus on the offering, not the outcome. By doing so, you will find it easier to feel peaceful and content in your heart.

I worked with a mother who was having a very difficult time with a teenaged daughter. The mother kept trying to "get" her daughter to be a "different person." The daughter refused. During one part of our working together, I asked the mother to adopt the "offerings" perspective rather than dwelling so much on how her daughter was turning out. That was tough because how her daughter turned out was so important to her. I could definitely understand that, being a parent myself. But she was finally willing to give it a try. I asked her to share with me each week the things she had decided to "offer" her daughter in specific terms by actually writing them down in a small notebook she carried. Basically, she was writing down the answer to, "What am I going to offer my daughter this week?" Some examples of what this mother offered to her daughter over time were the following:

- Suggesting that her daughter invite friends over for a video and treats the mother would provide to show interest in her friends and personal life.

- Talking with some of the teachers at her daughter's school to request they reach out to her and establish more of a relationship with her so someone else could help her rather than just her mother trying to do it alone.

- Sending the daughter a card or making a dessert she especially liked or doing some other thoughtful action to demonstrate every so often that she cared for her daughter, even when she was not always doing the things her mother hoped she would do.

The mother did not do these things without also trying her best to be clear on what her daughter needed to do to straighten out her life, but the mother felt, after making offerings like these, that she was also helping to bring some upbeat and encouraging influences into her daughter's life.

We did this for quite some time as one aspect of her counseling. I once even suggested that the best gift she could offer that particular week was to offer nothing. "Let your daughter experience life on her own," I said. "See what she learns from that." After a few months, I asked her to show me her notebook. We thumbed through the pages together, taking note of the myriad of items she had "offered" to her daughter. We were both impressed by how much she had offered with so little initial expectation of a good result. Interestingly, the daughter did make some changes and was doing somewhat better, although "better" was not even close to meeting the ideal expectations of her mother. But the mother was learning to look at what she had offered her daughter. She was also beginning to feel significant satisfaction regarding it. She had taken some big steps in looking at what she could do differently for her daughter. If she had remained fixated on how her daughter turned out, she would have felt disappointment at the end of her experiment.

As a parent, remember that you are helping to build a person; you are not simply achieving your own goals. Your child doesn't feel ultimately responsible to you or for you; rather, he feels responsible to and for himself. That is what you want anyway. After all, you won't always be around. Your child will need to learn to trust himself. At the symbolic altar you can talk, share, teach, and support; but then you must turn and walk away and let your child do his own work.

THE RISK FACTOR

Is this risky? Sure it is. Could you lose a child this way? Or at least have to stand by while something important fails? I imagine so. But things can go awry with a child no matter how you approach it. Let your child have the credit rather than taking it from her. Sometimes this approach will not produce the results you want. Your child may fall flat on her face. That is hard to watch. If it happens, seek to help her learn from her experience and go back to the drawing board. Sometimes you *both* will be wiser from the experience. Sometimes it will seem that she hasn't learned anything from a given experience. Just remember that learning may come later.

I have taught the altar approach to many parents. Some have tried it and then written me letters later reporting that they felt more peace in their lives and in their parenting. They reported that they were happier and enjoyed parenting more by offering their children what they could and then leaving the work and direction of things up to their children. The children also reported liking it better. They felt less pressured, less intimidated, more competent, and more trusted, so outcomes were often better! Some parents said it was a better approach even if it did not always work in terms of results. I think they got the idea.

I've used teenagers for most of my examples here, but this approach works with younger children as well, especially when they're eager to learn such everyday tasks as bed making, dish washing, and even feeding themselves. Let your children try, even if the outcome will be "messy." Let your young children make choices and decisions that are reasonable for their age. This will help them feel more competent. The underlying principle is the same: *Give me room to try unless I prove that I can't handle it. But don't take away my choices out of fear that I will disappoint you or make you look like you are not doing a good job as parents or simply make a mess in your kitchen.* As children grow toward adulthood they need to experiment with autonomy. Growing competence has a certain amount of personal miscalculation in it. A child won't make the bed as well as Mommy and Daddy can, but if you let her try, she may learn to believe in herself. There is nothing better, at any age, than to hear these words from your parent, "*You* did it!"

A child won't make the bed as well as Mommy and Daddy can, but if you let her try, she may learn to believe in herself.

A Correct Principle

Parents in more functional families ponder over what they want for each child in their family. But they don't leave it there. They get busy and work at it. More functional families have more active parents.

More functional families also have parents who can sit back and watch, hoping for the outcomes they sought after. More functional families have parents who realize that they can't fully control outcomes—nor do they really want to. They know they can put all they want into whatever they choose to offer their children. It is like a putt in golf. You line it up and, from several angles, consider how you will stroke it. Then you strike the ball. And once you've done this you can no longer control whether or not it will go into the hole. This approach requires a fundamental trust in what I term the "real work of parenting." The real work of parenting involves the following:

- Regularly holding Family Discussion Time with your spouse.
- Spending FDT thinking about and discussing your children.
- Determining what you will offer your children, and how you will offer it.
- Making the offering—for it is the offering that counts most.

So, go hold an FDT. Offer something to your children and then let them go on their personal journey. Give it a try and see what happens.

I know you are still thinking about results to some degree. If your offering does not get you close enough to the result you hoped for, take the situation back to FDT for an adjustment—another try. Keep refocusing and trying. Consult with your partner. Work together on it.

Rate yourself on the concept of emphasizing offerings rather than outcomes._____

What steps do you need to take to strengthen your parenting in this area?

CHAPTER 6

Intentional Parenting Is Crucial

One Saturday Sherri and I were racing around, trying to get to all of our children's soccer games. The confusion seemed endless. We had five games to get to between 8 A.M. and noon. She and I had decided which of the games each of us would go to (while hauling some of the littlest kids with us!) and found that there was one we simply couldn't make! I remember saying to Sherri, "They know we try hard to get there. It won't matter if we miss one." But it bugged me to death to think that one of our little ones would be scanning the sidelines, looking for his mom and dad, and not finding one of us! To help prevent any real disappointment, we sent one of our teenagers to watch that game. We got *someone* to every game for at least part of the time. Why did we try so hard? Because Sherri and I had already decided that supporting our children was one of our strongest commitments. We wanted our children to feel as if we were standing in front of them holding up a huge sign with big letters that read, "YOU ARE SO IMPORTANT TO US THAT WE ARE HERE. WE LOVE YOU!"

If you're reading this book, it's probably because you love your kids and are looking for some new ideas on how to be a better parent. You want your kids to feel they have parents close by who are holding up signs of support. You've probably found many ways to do this in your own life. One of the best ways I've found to do this is to make an intentional effort to be a parent. Action is the key. Active parenting simply means that you pick an area within your parent-child relationship and work on it. To bring this idea into everyday life I recommend you sit down in Family Discussion Time, take out a piece of paper, and each answer this question: "What are three areas within our family relationships where I personally could go to work to make a significant difference?" Then share your answers with each other. I love to see parents taking some FDT to brainstorm and come up with great stuff to try out in the family. ACTIVE parents—I love it! Let me warn you that the rest of this chapter offers lots of ideas on how to be actively involved in your family. There is likely way more than you can or want to do. Read it over and then choose a few good ideas to try out. You don't need to do it all at once! Try out some of your ideas and evaluate yourself again two or three weeks later. Then just evaluate from time to time after that. You'll find that intentional efforts can really pay off.

For example, suppose you are working hard to build up relationships with family members. Initially you rate yourself as a 4 on the ten-scale, which indicates that you need to do some significant work on building relationships in your family. After working on relationships for a period of time, you do a new ten-scale evaluation and find that you've moved up to a 6. You're very likely to feel a lot better at 6 than you did at 4. You like feeling better, so you decide to push on to 7 or 8. At this point, you need to ask yourself specifically what to do to get to 7 or 8. This pattern for improvement—identifying something to try out, evaluating yourself, practicing some more, reevaluating, and then continuing to practice and further evaluate until you get where you want to be— works so well because it builds upon progress little by little rather than tackling everything at once and setting yourself up for disappointment. Active approaches to change in the family require that you ask yourself, "What can I do to actively make a difference in my family?" and wrestle to find answers. This approach—and the ten-scale, specifically—help you do that.

Active approaches to change in the family require that you ask yourself questions and wrestle to answer them.

THE IMPACT YOU HAVE ON YOUR CHILDREN

I love coming across parents who "parent" each child individually and intentionally. These parents are definitely aware of the great impact they can have on their children. Their parental influence really matters to them. They may even ask questions such as, "How do I influence my children?" "Do I consciously and beneficially impact each one of them?" "How do I know if I am having a positive and desirable influence on my children?" These are always great Family Discussion Time topics.

Let me share an example with you. I'll call this family the Petersons. Mr. and Mrs. Peterson have two children, ages twelve and ten, and they have recently perceived that both children need some help with challenges they are facing.

In the past, their son Justin hasn't brought up problems or

concerns very quickly. The Petersons know it might take time before he tells them what's bothering him. They decide that just being there for him is enough until he can open up. To show that they care, they decide to go to each of Justin's baseball games together so that he knows both his parents are available and interested in him. Perhaps he will seek their help later. They've learned that, for Justin, it's best to do more with the relationship *before* trying to problem solve.

With Aaron, however, they take another route. In Family Discussion Time they decide that Dad will take time to sit down and talk with Aaron. Mr. Peterson will ask Aaron about the difficulty he is facing and help him pursue some solutions. Mr. and Mrs. Peterson have correctly perceived in the past that Aaron is a very open child and is typically anxious to receive help. His problem is similar to Justin's, but the solution requires a different approach.

Like the Peterson boys, your children have come to you as different individuals, and they will each respond to your parenting differently. You've probably already tried the same thing with two children and gotten completely different responses. You may be successful with one but see the whole process go more slowly and less effectively with another. Individual differences in family members sure are fun! They require that you *intentionally* parent *each* child.

So, how do you intentionally influence your children? How do you influence them in significant ways but not overwhelm them? You need a time and place to work on it. The key time and place is Family Discussion Time. By committing yourself to hold that regular meeting you are creating a time and place to think and plan for your family. This practice is one of the most important things you do each week in your family. It is essential in the operation of the more functional family. During FDT, stop and ask yourself, "How do I want to influence my family?" Or, "How do I want to influence Michael or Alexis?"

You still have your pad of paper in front of you for writing down your thoughts and plans, right? This is more important than any contract you are writing up at work! Wait till you see this next idea. One of the best!

THE BLACKBOARD CONCEPT

You probably recall the blackboard I referred to in chapter 3. Taking that concept and turning it into a positive and useful tool in parenting has helped me more, on a daily basis, in influencing my children than almost anything I can think of. Here is how it works. Imagine that each of your children carries around a *personal blackboard*. What purpose does it serve? It is there so that you as a parent can write messages on it about that particular child. It is as if your child is standing there holding up her blackboard, saying to you, "Write on it what you think of me. Write on it what you want me to think of myself." The potential of what you can communicate to a child is powerful. What message would you like to write on it today? This requires that you know something about your child. You need to know where she is in life, and what she might need help with. You can assume that she needs certain things like love, for example. (I write about that part of the blackboard concept in a later chapter.) It is a fascinating experience to spend some time thinking about your child and determining what you do or do not know about her. This is in preparation for writing messages on her personal blackboard.

Knowing that every child has an essential need for love from the moment she takes her first breath, I write a love letter to each of my grandchildren on the day he or she is born. I tell them about our family and how thrilled we are that they have joined us. I tell about their parents and what wonderful people they are. I tell them how crazy I am but that I am sure they can handle it. I remember when Allyson was born. She received her love letter from Grandpa Sparky (that is my nickname) in the mail right away. Her mother told me later, "She even stopped eating while I read it to her!" Why did I write that letter to Allyson? I knew she had a personal blackboard, and I wanted to write on it immediately!

Take a sheet of paper and write, at the top, the name of one of your children. Underneath that write what you know about her. How old is she? What is she doing in life right now? Does she need help? From whom? Why? In what areas? Does she need help from you as her parent? Why? How will you help her get it? How does your child feel about herself? Is she happy? Secure? Self-confident? Struggling? Does she come across different publicly from how she really feels privately? The underlying question is this: How much do you know about your child? Maybe you will be surprised to realize you are not certain about the answer to a number of things that pertain to her. That may give you some insight into your relationship with that particular child.

How can you discover the answers to these questions? How can you get to know your child? With one child you might feel the best thing to do is to simply ask her about what is going on in her life. For another that will be too direct. You may need to patiently observe and take the time to learn about her by "hanging out" with her more than you do now. You can sometimes learn a lot about a person while bowling, playing golf, or going to lunch together. Try canceling something if you can, and then call one of your children to go with you to the mall one afternoon. She might be happily shocked! You need contact to know a person, even someone in your very own family. *If the relationship feels right,* conversations occur and things happen. With some effort on your part, you can learn about your child and get to know her better than you do now. Along with that, you may need to be honest and say, "I have not taken the time to get to know you very well. I want to improve on that."

I have had many parents tell me that they regularly make active interventions on projects at work, digging into them and finding out what needs to be done to make a project work. It shocks them to realize they don't do it at home, where finding out about family members is significantly more important in the larger scope of things.

Don't worry too much if you chose one approach with a child and it doesn't work perfectly. If you are in the middle of an attempt that isn't working, you can always say something like, "I am interested in you and wanted to show my interest better than I have in the past. Maybe you can give me some help on this." It may shock your child, but it shows sincere interest. Your attempts to actively and intentionally parent your children don't need to be written up in the newspaper to be noteworthy. Almost anything you attempt will be better than if you had not tried.

Why am I suggesting all this "get to know the child" stuff? Because knowing your child well helps you write on her blackboard. That means you have done your "homework" and have an idea about what you can do to positively influence your child's life. With a much clearer picture of your child you now begin to write on her personal blackboard. You write messages on her blackboard that you feel will be of benefit to her based upon what you have learned about her. Let's discuss those messages for a little bit, both the *negative* and the *positive* messages.

NEGATIVE MESSAGES

Sometimes it becomes painfully clear to a parent that what he needs to do is to *stop* writing certain messages on a child's blackboard. Perhaps a parent regularly writes messages that are demeaning and humiliating—he is being too critical of his child. By the parent's simply recognizing and then stopping such comments, the relationship may begin to improve.

Your child's blackboard receives negative messages from many sources. Some are unintentional, but they still have a powerful impact on your child. Some are intentional and are subsequently very destructive. Some are written by people outside the home; you can't always do much about those but help your child understand why they happen and how to deal with them. In general, however, parents have the most power to influence their children positively or negatively. You have a great responsibility to take time to think about what you are communicating to your children.

Watch out for negative patterns in what you say and do in your relationship with your children. What is a negative pattern? It is something that may appear on your children's blackboard that has a harmful effect on them and happens *repeatedly*. It is like a hammer hitting a nail. Pound, pound, pound. Over and over it strikes. Negative patterns can dig deep holes, causing significant damage.

I once gave a talk about negative patterns, and a parent came up afterwards to tell me an insight she had while listening to me. She reported that she constantly said to one of her daughters, "What is the matter with you?" Previously, she thought she had a right to say that. She was the mother and she needed to cause her daughter to think. Now it struck her that she was repeatedly reminding her daughter that her mother felt there was something fundamentally wrong with her. She needed to find some other way to get her daughter to think. Using that question had too much negative fallout.

If you want to know if you are contributing to any such negative patterns in your children's lives, ask someone you trust to observe you and let you know if they see anything like that occurring in your family relationships. Maybe they will tell you, and you can then become more aware of your own negative patterns in family relationships. Some of the most common negative patterns are criticizing, yelling and screaming, humiliating or belittling, neglecting or ignoring, being sarcastic, teasing or making fun of others, showing anger, name calling, rejecting, fighting, withdrawing love, and being impatient. Lots to avoid, huh? I call these things *relationship busters,* and they can put damaging messages on your children's blackboards, even if that is not your intention.

Some time ago I had a counseling session with a client whose self-image had been strongly dominated by a series of experiences with her father. This father had consistently communicated that my client was physically unattractive. I actually thought she was above average in physical appearance. During one counseling session, I asked her to identify an aspect of her physical self that she found acceptable. With great difficulty she said, "Some people think my eyes are okay."

"Only okay?" I said to her.

"Only okay, and I have only heard that from one or two people." It became obvious that she had denied any positive contradiction to her father's view. It would take a lot of difficult work to expand her view of herself and free her from the powerful impact of her father's words and actions. He had written on her blackboard, "You are not attractive," far too often.

In this case a negative message was *etched* into the child's blackboard, making it very difficult to erase. That is why we need to be careful about such messages.

The ability to refrain from such interactions within family relationships comes easier when you understand what such messages do to your children. Let's take the negative patterns we have identified and translate them into words that show you what each one can end up writing on your child's blackboard. Then *you* can decide if you want to keep that pattern or get rid of it. Each is described boldly so you get the full potential negative impact of each one.

Following are ten-scale self-evaluations to help you to see to what degree you might be employing these negative messages in your parent-child relationships. You can do it child by child (if you have more than one) or for your children as a group.

Criticizing

"You make so many mistakes. I have to fix you because you are not acceptable as you are."_____

Yelling and screaming

"You are weak, and I can dominate you. There is something wrong with you, and that is why I don't like you."_____

Humiliating and belittling

"You are worthless. You are an embarrassment to me. Sometimes I actually want you to feel small and insignificant."_____

Neglecting and ignoring

"You are not important to me, and you are not wanted. You get in the way of my doing more important things."_____

Being sarcastic

"I talk to you in a demeaning way because I am trying to put you down where you belong."_____

Teasing and making fun of another

"I am covering up my negative feelings for you by trying to

make it funny. But I am putting you down because you deserve to be put down." _____

Showing anger

"I don't like you. I need to punish you, control you, and put you down."_____

Rejecting

"I don't want you. I don't like you. There is something wrong with you."_____

Fighting

"You are like an enemy to me. If you were not so disappointing, I would not have to defeat you and put you in your place."_____

Withdrawing of love

"If you do not do what I say and obey me, you must pay for it by losing my love."_____

Being impatient

"I cannot tolerate you. You make so many mistakes. You have too many flaws in you."_____

As you read the messages these negative patterns communicate, did you notice how often the idea "something is wrong with you" came up? These negative patterns are vicious largely because they cause the persons receiving them to question something fundamental about themselves.

Look at the list again. Did you find any areas that really concern you? Any *red flags* that you need to work on? Red-flag areas are 7 or higher on the ten-scale. List your red-flag concerns and then discuss them in Family Discussion Time. Remember that most of us have to work hard not to exhibit the patterns listed above. Even if you identified three or four areas as "red flags," you still have eight or nine areas that are not! If you find areas where your ten-scale assessments are quite low (a 1, 2, or 3, for example), call those your *white flags*. White-flag areas indicate strength in how you treat your children. What red or white flags do you have?

Red Flags

1.

2.

3.

White Flags

1.

2.

3.

If anything has helped me to reevaluate how I speak to my children and how I treat them, it has been understanding the "voice" they hear when I engage in the negative patterns just described. It hurts me to think that my own messages to my children are in any way similar to these negative "voices." I don't want to be part of the tearing down of my children. I want to be a part of building them up and edifying them.

Positive Messages

The human spirit responds to that which ennobles. Your child likes to be nourished, just as you do. There is a series of ennobling interventions you can make in your child's daily life and thus nourish his spirit. Courtesy provides nourishment. Love does. Respect and kindness do. Listening does. Service, sacrifice, compliments, and forgiveness do. Any good and positive emotion can help you nurture your child. Take an opportunity to nourish your child with one of those ennobling interventions. See how you feel and how your child feels after a day or two of writing on his blackboard with an ennobling pen. Such choices on your part usually produce many, many ennobling and uplifting messages on the child's blackboard. Children love to read these messages.

In practical terms, I actually like to write down on a piece of paper the message I want my child to read on his blackboard. On the paper next to the message, I write down some things I can actually do to make that message come alive in the mind of my child. For example, I write, "My dad thinks highly of me" (message I want to have appear on his blackboard). Then next to it I write several things I can do to get that message across, such as, "Tell him that I am very proud of his performance in school," or "Tell him I want him to play the piano for us at a family get-together," or "Tell the family at Family Evenings about his shoveling snow off the neighbor's sidewalk and driveway."

You can also *do* something rather than say something. The message "My dad thinks highly of me" can be written on a child's blackboard by going to watch him play soccer or by playing a game with him. Or you could communicate that message by having an informal chat with him. In that chat you could ask for his opinion or for him to help you figure something out. At the conclusion of the chat you could say something like, "You have a good mind. Thanks for helping me." That is how it works. You identify the message you want your child to receive, and then you explore what you can do to help your child actually receive that message.

One parent did this with at least one child regularly for

several months. During that time she kept it all written down in her family notebook. Later she read over all the things she had decided to do during that period of time. It really made her feel good to know that she had focused on her children in such specific and helpful ways for so long. She could see what she had done over time. She had made a concerted effort to influence things positively. For that she felt a sense of great satisfaction. Focusing on offerings rather than outcomes, she had "offered" a lot over time.

Not all efforts produce the desired impact, of course, but making continued efforts will help you feel much better about your parenting efforts. You may be impatient for results. Sometimes the results do come, but they are not always the results you expected. In the final analysis, all you can do is offer whatever you can and be grateful that you have decided to make regular and faithful efforts to make a difference in your children's lives.

Is there a theme you could emphasize with a certain child? Something you could do over and over again to inscribe a positive message on your child's blackboard? There most likely is, so give it a try. Practice some ennobling interventions. After a while, your child will most likely notice. The positive message will sink in, and your child will be the better for it. Some time ago I decided to work on regularly complimenting my young grandchildren. Since then, almost every time I see one of them I will tell her, "You are cute and smart." I want my grandchildren to hear this message over and over. They like it now, and they'll come to believe it if I just keep at it.

"You are cute and smart." I want my grandchildren to hear this message over and over. They like it now, and they'll come to believe it if I just keep at it.

Following are ten-scale self-evaluations to help you to see to what degree you might be employing these positive messages in your parent-child relationships. You can do it child by child (if you have more than one) or for your children as a group.

Love

"I care about you and want you to feel your full value and significance to me."_____

Respect and kindness

"I want you to feel how good and wonderful you are in my eyes."_____

Listening

"I want to focus on and acknowledge you to show you are worth it to me."_____

Service

"I want to give of myself to you so you can feel your own sense of personal value and worth to me."_____

Sacrifice

"I want to give up something for you so you will know how important you are to me."_____

Compliments

"I want to highlight how good and capable you are."

_____

A GREAT GUIDING CONCEPT

Once you understand the impact of positive and negative message patterns, you have a great concept to guide you in your everyday parent-child interaction. At almost any point in the day I can stop, think of one of my children, and ask myself, "What message could I put on _____'s blackboard today, and how will I do it?" Quite simple. Very practical. It really works. I still do it regularly in my own family, and my children are all older than twenty. I do it with other people too. Everyone has a blackboard and wants to find uplifting messages written on it. Help all of them out.

Before you start analyzing everything you've ever said and done, I should caution you to not become paranoid that every word can or will damage your child. We all make mistakes in our parenting, and our children mostly survive those mistakes. Individual errors in parenting are generally forgotten quickly and have little long-term effect (unless it is one single event that is very traumatic). You should be concerned about how you treat your children and what you write on their blackboards, but you should not become excessively preoccupied with every mistake you make. All parents are imperfect. That includes you! *Teach your children that you are imperfect and so are they.* It is a natural part of living. We all make our share of mistakes. We are here to learn from them. Mistakes are part of growing up and gaining wisdom and understanding as children and adults. Use this concept to guide you, not to drive you to insanity!

THE IMPACT OF THE OUTSIDE WORLD

Many sources outside the family also write on your children's blackboards. Your children might go to school and have someone write on their blackboards that they are undesirable or unwanted. They will then come home and walk in the house with that message on their blackboards. It influences how they feel about themselves. Pay attention to what you suspect is written on their blackboards while they are away from you—at school, on sports teams, and with their friends. Sometimes good messages are written on their blackboards and sometimes not. One of the most important things you can do during Family Discussion Time is to ask, "What messages have been written on our children's blackboards lately?"

It is crucial to pay attention to your children, to know them. You must know what the world out there is writing on your children's blackboards. In a weekly Family Evening, you might want to try this interesting experience. Set up a whiteboard and write on it, "What messages are written on teenagers' blackboards nowadays?" (Hopefully you have already taught your children about blackboards and how they work in the family, so a chat about this won't surprise them.) You might be surprised at all you learn from listening to your teenaged children answer this question.

To find out more about your children you might have to sit down with them *regularly* and talk about what goes on in their lives. What a great tradition to start when they are young. In our family, we used to call these times "interviews." They were not really interviews but chats in which I could find out how my children felt about what was going on in their lives. There are so many areas you can chat about. Take a look at school, sports, music lessons, friends, bad as well as good experiences, and things that make them happy, sad, mad, angry, frustrated, nervous, depressed, excited, confident, or worried. Don't use a checklist; children usually feel interrogated in such a setting. If the "chat" is too formal, it reduces the chance for enhancing the relationship. Conducting the "interview" over a bowl of ice cream usually works quite well.

Children will inevitably cooperate better with these chats when they are young, whereas it might be harder when they are older. If you can establish this as a family tradition when they are younger, it will feel natural as they get older. But people like to be cared about, so show sincere and regular interest.

Parents can get busy and fail to take time to notice their children. That happens to me; does it to you? A great thing to do is to just watch a particular child, more than you usually would, for a day and see what you learn. At Family Discussion Time one of the great experiences you can have as parents is to compare notes on what you think is going on with each child and what is being written on their blackboards outside and inside the family. Use the ten-scale here. It will help you compare notes. One of you may view a given child at 3 on a ten-scale in a certain area (low) and the other parent a 5 (a moderate rating). To discuss why you gave different ratings can give you much deeper understanding of what your child experiences daily. Just the fact that you are taking some time to talk about your family members individually is wonderful! This demonstrates that you are "tuned in" to their lives.

As you become aware of what the outside world is writing on your child's blackboard, you can consider together how to place competing messages on that child's blackboard. Don't let possible negative outside influences take over. Resist them. *Act in behalf of your child in a conscious way.* If you take this effort seriously, you can agree to come to Family Discussion Time with impressions written down and you can see how your perceptions of the family compare with those of your partner. Does this sound like an awful lot of work? It does take work. But it can be meaningful work. FDT is a time for you and your spouse to be together, just the two of you. The plans you make in FDT allow you opportunities to interact with your children and really get to know them, something that might not happen if you just let life take over and didn't intervene.

I'll say it over and over: Honestly, nothing you will do in a given week is more important than regularly holding a well-thought-out Family Discussion Time. Suppose you come to FDT and say to your spouse, "I have been thinking about Mark. He seems angry lately. He is easily offended and snaps at people in the family. What do you think is going on with him?" You share some thoughts and attempt to be clear on what you know about Mark. Once you get a fix on the answer to the first question, then you move on to the follow-up question, which is, "What do you think we can do to help him? What shall we write on his blackboard?"

Nothing you will do in a given week is more important than regularly holding a well-thought-out Family Discussion Time.

If you are a single parent, you will need to tune in to what you yourself have noticed. Then what do you do? Though I know your time is very limited, my strongest recommendation for single parents is to find another single parent who would get together with you to think through your plans regarding your children. This will give you someone who can react to your ideas and insights. No one likes to do this alone. Team up! Maybe a short phone call or email could help you support each other in this way.

Your goal is to decide what to do to write new "inside messages" on that blackboard—messages that will counter those from outside the family that are troublesome and potentially destructive. In Family Discussion Time, talk about how to enlist others in the family in writing on a certain family member's blackboard. For example, if you have a child struggling in school, you might take a trip to meet with your child's teacher to let her know what you are observing and what you think will help. Or you may decide to get a tutor. Or you could spend extra time doing homework with that child. You could also have some fun together later so school doesn't get too burdensome or have too much influence on her self-esteem. Those are all great ways of writing on a child's blackboard.

If you understand this principle, you are not helpless, regardless of the messages other people write on her blackboard. Following this principle gives you something to do as parents that allows you to feel you can make a difference. Please remember the previous chapter on doing what you can to offer something that will influence your child's life, rather than getting too hung up on the results of your efforts. Every parent can do something that can influence his or her children's lives beneficially. Though I am sure this sounds like more work than you can do, you don't have to do all of it by any means. Look over these ideas and pick one or two to try out. Do what you can, given your own unique personal circumstances.

And you can always stop and ask yourself, "What message does my child need on her blackboard right now, and how can I help get it there?" It may take repeated efforts at writing on that child's blackboard to begin to see a difference. Blackboards beware! Mom and Dad are coming your way! We will not give up easily! We have lots of chalk, and we will be working on it regularly at Family Discussion Time.

So how do you know that any of this makes a difference? You don't always know. Patience helps. You may not be certain. You observe. If it seems appropriate, you can even ask your child about a certain aspect of her life to see if what you are attempting to do is making any difference. You can see what others observe. Sometimes you just offer and hope for the result you want. Some parents have told me they kept writing on a child's blackboard long into her adult life before the desired effects became apparent. Don't lose hope. The worst thing is to stop. Keep your chalk ready. Write. Then be available to write some more and do every-thing you can to be a positive influence on your child.

Rate yourself on the concept of making intentional efforts to influence your children, keeping in mind the blackboard concept._____

What steps do you need to take to implement this concept into your parenting?

CHAPTER 7

The Parental Mission–
Building Healthy
Children

When each of our grandchildren is born, almost all of the family shows up at the hospital and waits for the new little one's arrival, no matter the time of day. I think this is great. I like the family atmosphere that surrounds each birth. At one of these events, I mentioned to an older son that I was very impressed so many would come to the birth of a baby! He said, "I think we all want our names in his baby book . . . and I bet it will help him know how important he is to us, even on the first day of his life." I thought I would cry. I think I did.

One of the major purposes in a more functional family is to create an environment and atmosphere that foster healthy emotional development in family members. The parents take the lead in this effort, recognizing that the family is a *workshop* where healthy people are built. Knowing the essential building blocks of a healthy human being is crucial as you work at building people in your families. There are few efforts more important than thoughtfully working toward the healthy development of your children.

What would it be like if, in every home, every parent considered the building of healthy children to be his or her first and greatest priority? What would society's homes and families be like? How would they change? I believe our homes would be transformed before our very eyes.

ESSENTIAL BUILDING BLOCKS OF A HEALTHY PERSON

What are the essential ingredients, or the main building blocks, of a healthy person? I'll review them here. And, after I do, I hope that you will talk about your children and do a ten-scale assessment on each one to see how he or she is doing in these areas. Fulfillment of basic human needs is what we all desire at our core. Food, water, and air are essential to our physical well-being. But there are also personal and emotional needs that are just as essential. When these needs are not met, we tend to demonstrate stressful and negative characteristics. Human beings want to feel good about who they are.

Need #1: Every person wants to feel significant and valuable

How important is it to you to feel personally significant and valuable? I believe everyone wants to feel that way. Sometimes a person will acknowledge it, and sometimes he will not. I am convinced, however, that this need lies at the heart of every person. To be able to say, "I feel significant and valuable in my family," is what family members are seeking. Everyone wants to feel a certain amount of fundamental worth that exists independent of how well he performs. That aspect of worth is not earned; it is granted.

Individuals in healthy families learn that by being alive, they get to be valued. These are called primary feelings of worth. If family members accept each other as always possessing a certain fundamental level of significance and value, then they know they can't ever be of "no value." Along with that comes an additional, or supplemental, amount of worth that *is* a product of what each person does. That is also important. I refer to that as worth through competence. To explore competence further, refer to Need #3 below.

Need #2: Every person wants to feel loved

Everyone wants to be cared about and loved. In the family, love should be inevitable, ingrained into the woodwork of family life and etched into the unwritten rules of what a family is. Individuals who feel they will be cared about only *after* they change or perform a certain way feel rejected. Placing a price tag on love creates anxiety. But if love is freely offered, the individual knows that her performance is carried out for some other reward, not for love. If she doesn't perform adequately, she may lose a certain amount of personal growth or satisfaction, but she will *not* lose something that lies at the core of her life—love. Talk about this in the family. Agree that this is how your family will operate. It is a decision you make together.

You may want your children to change in certain ways, but each one must also feel loved as she is.

Some things in life should just be free. They should not be based on meeting certain conditions. They are too fundamental to human well-being to be earned. Feeling loved is one of them. You may want your children to change in certain ways, but each one must also feel loved as she is. In the family, individuals commit to loving one another through good times and bad. To feel cared about provides a form of security that is important to emotional well-being. When you feel emotionally secure and safe, *then* you can work at change and growth without so much anxiety. In other words, receiving dependable love first helps you find the strength to pursue change, if that is needed. When we experience this type of love, feelings of personal worth usually follow. The message of such love is "I feel loved. I must be worth it." To know you are a person of worth is one thing; to feel it, through being loved, is another. In the more functional family, feelings of worth and feelings of being loved are indelibly linked.

Need #3: Every person wants to feel capable and competent

Individuals need to feel that they can undertake and carry out new tasks. Engaging in new opportunities in life is a key to potential growth. To be able to look at this world of possibility and feel optimistic and confident about your abilities allows you to grow and develop, to try new and sometimes hard things.

> *Part of an individual's personal worth and value is free, without conditions, and part is earned by how he performs.*

Experiencing feelings of competence, which are a product of being able to do certain things well enough, helps develop additional feelings of worth. So part of an individual's personal worth and value is free, without conditions, and part is earned by how he performs. Leaving out the first part, and thus believing all personal worth is earned, results in anxiety. If, however, an individual has a foundation of personal worth—one that came at no cost to him—he can't drop to a level of "no worth." That free foundation of personal worth is what individuals in healthy families build on as they learn, grow, and progress in life. The free part of worth is like a cake, and the earned part is like the frosting on the cake.

As I have observed children's levels of self-esteem, I have found a correlation between worth and feelings of competency and capability. It is crucial that parents ask this question: What can I do, given the age of my child, to help him develop skills, abilities, capabilities, strengths, and talents? Anything you can do to consistently work at building such things in your child will contribute immensely to his development as a person. Offer him all the opportunities you can to try out new things.

In the more functional family, parents know that they must do all they can to create healthy "soil" in which their children can grow to adulthood and thus feel capable and competent. They know that such healthy emotional soil is essential to the well-being of family members. In the more functional family, parents work to be sure that rich family soil is readily available. Members in healthy families report such feelings as the following:

I feel important here.

I feel valuable here.

I feel significant here.

I feel worthwhile here.

I feel loved here.

I feel capable here.

People like feeling these things. To be personally healthy, they *need* to be able to feel these things. I believe that the family's fundamental reason for existence is to nurture family members and help them build personal optimism about themselves. The six "I feel" statements above can guide your parental thinking and your actions in the family. For example, if you have no pressing issues to discuss in Family Discussion Time, cycle through these six statements, checking out (ten-scale, of course) how various family members are doing relative to each feeling.

Keep in mind, as you work in your family to address these crucial needs, that what you offer can also be taken less seriously than you intended, or even rejected. Acceptance of love and guidance is a decision on the part of the receiver.

Also, keep in mind the extremely important fact that children can help other children in the family experience feelings like the six listed above. You are the leaders in the family, but you do not have to do it all by yourselves. Some of the most unforgettable experiences I have seen parents experience in guiding their families came after they enlisted the help of another child in the family. Try asking one child for suggestions that would benefit a sibling: "Mary is struggling at school because she doesn't have many friends. Do you have some suggestions on what we could do as a family to help her?"

Some of the most unforgettable experiences I have seen parents experience in guiding their families came after they enlisted the help of another child in the family.

I would like to share here one very personal belief about mothers and their contribution in this area of family life. The world today does not pay adequate respect to mothers. Mothers are life-givers. They know something about the giving of life that a man does not know. It is part of being a mother to breathe life into her children's lives. I believe mothers are called upon to be nurturers. Fathers should nurture too, but mothers possess a special gift in this area of family life. They can help children feel and experience the six "I feel" statements in very unique ways. Their mission is to teach these things. They are born to give life to such beliefs and feelings in the minds and hearts of their children. I believe that. I honor mothers for their gifts, talents, and dedication in these important areas of family life. We need more mothers doing what mothers do best.

Interestingly, most family members have a favorite way of being loved. It's easier for an individual to receive and welcome love offered in her own preferred way. Try writing down the way in which you think each of your family members feels most loved. You might find, in some cases, that you don't know! If you don't know, give your child *time filled with interest.* Little you can give each other in the family is more powerful than the gift of time, laden with personal interest. It says, "I am here for you. I give you my time."

Little you can give each other in the family is more powerful than the gift of time, laden with personal interest. It says, "I am here for you. I give you my time."

Sometimes, asking others in the family about a particular family member will help you get some good ideas. You might say to another family member, "I would like to get closer to Ben. What do you think helps him feel cared about in our family?"

Another action that is likely to have a positive effect on almost anyone in your family is to do something *thoughtful.* Send a card in the mail, for example, or put up a love note on the mirror in her bedroom, take her out to lunch, do a fun activity together, spend some time talking, buy her a special treat and bring it home to her, or even make her bed.

Thoughtful means you are "full of thought" about a certain person. Somehow, showing a family member that you are thinking of her by paying attention to her carries with it a strong message of positive regard. Recently I sent an email to one of my adult sons. It read simply, "You are cool." I wanted him to know I was thinking about him. About two hours later I got an email back. It said, "You are too." I loved knowing that I was "thought about." I think he did too.

One last word of advice on this topic: Don't be afraid to guess about how a particular family member feels loved! One of the best "guesses" may be simply saying, "I love you." For those who are struggling, the words "I love you" can sweep away pain and unhappiness, even if only for a brief time. Say it again and again. Most children—and spouses—like hearing it.

The Big Three

We each have a deep and abiding need to feel worthwhile and to know that we count for something. We all want to feel that we have value in our own eyes as well as in the eyes of others. We desperately want to know that we are loved. We also want to feel we can deal with the world competently. I remember a client telling me once, "I hate feeling incompetent!" I told him I hated that feeling too. Feelings of personal incompetence are a threat to self-esteem. People who live without feelings of competence do much more poorly in life overall. So, your quest as a parent is to ask yourself, "How do I help each of my children to feel significant, loved, and competent?" These are the *big three*.

The vital requisites for sound emotional health are bought with a price that parents must be willing to pay. The currency with which they are bought is time, attention, interest, effort, and sacrifice.

When our children were quite young, they participated in a children's program at our church called Primary. In Primary, the children were occasionally asked to say a "part" (just a few words for the very little ones) or give a "talk" (probably 2 or 3 minutes in length). When the family would come home from church on the day of the "talk," we would put the child who did the part or the talk up on the kitchen table, award him *two* treats, and then applaud. Everyone else in the family got one treat, too, just for being there.

It was a family event. Can you see *significant, loved,* and *competent* in that scene? People always wondered why our children volunteered to give talks and do parts! Did the treats do it? I think they helped, but I also think it was the loving attention paid to them as competent people that they desired most.

These vital requisites—"the big three"—for sound emotional health are bought with a price that parents must be willing to pay. The currency with which they are bought is *time, attention, interest, effort,* and *sacrifice.* A friend of ours recently shared this family experience: "One afternoon our young son was very distraught over being unable to understand a difficult math problem. He had a big test the next day, and he had to understand how to do that problem or he would do poorly on the test. His father came in from work on the run, needing to prepare an important professional talk to give the next day in another state. Not only did he need to prepare his talk but he had to get ready to travel and leave on a plane early the next morning.

"As he came through the front door, our son stopped him and asked him to *please* help him with the math problem he *had* to understand for his big test the next day. He knew nothing of his father's own stress over preparing the talk and getting ready to travel. His dad sat down with him, saying nothing about his own situation, and began to work the math problem. He couldn't figure it out. Finally, our son went off to bed, and his dad continued to work on the math problem."

The next morning when the boy woke up, he found on the desk in his bedroom the completed problem with an explanation of how to do it. At the top of the note to his son, his dad wrote: "It is 3 A.M. I am packing to leave on my trip, so I won't be here to talk this over with you in the morning. I hope this helps you on your test. Love, Dad."

Interestingly, the wife traveled later in the day to hear her husband give his speech. She observed that it was not one of his best. And she was the only one in the audience who knew why— because he had spent the evening and half the night working out the math problem for his son. Then she made a statement that I will never forget: "It is now years later, and no one remembers that not-so-well-prepared speech my husband gave that day, but our son has never forgotten his father's sacrifice to help him with something that was very important to a young teenaged boy. There is a lesson about families in my husband's decision to care about and help his son."

What level of devotion and commitment did you experience from your own parents as you were growing up? How did it affect you? Is there anything in family life more important than commitment to your children and their well-being? It is parental commitment that nourishes and inspires the next generation. Some who read this may wonder if they can make such a commitment—of time, attention, interest, effort, and sacrifice. Take heart! Remember the wonderful ten-scale! You don't need to be a 10 on a ten-scale in each of those areas. Try starting with a 6 or a 7 and work from there.

How You Spend Your Time

As you begin working on the "big three," try evaluating how you spend your time related to the family. Have you ever actually kept track of where your time goes, even when you are physically in the home? In my practice, I see many parents who are not at home or with their families very much. Their children sometimes feel ignored and less loved. I also see parents who are physically present, but their children still feel ignored and less loved! Why? You can guess. Some parents are physically present but psychologically absent. They are in the home but not emotionally available to their children. Often there is little parent-child interaction. Some parents are so tired from their work schedules that they arrive home with little left in their personal reservoirs. All parents know what it feels like to be a tired parent. Busy schedules and expectations make for complex lives and many reasons for being away from the home. None of us can up and quit our jobs or do anything else that dramatic. So, what can you do to spend more time with your children? I think the first thing you can do is recognize the consequences of being less available to your family. Talk them over with your spouse in Family Discussion Time and see if there are new ways to manage your time and be even just a little more available to your family.

A neighbor shared with me this tender experience of a dad who tried his best. He was working a full-time job and two part-time jobs to keep things together economically for his family. One evening he came in about 8 P.M. from his second job to have a quick bite to eat en route to his other part-time job, which went late into the night. He was exhausted. But he had hardly seen his children in days. He was well aware of the consequences of his continued absence, but felt compelled to continue his extra jobs. He was frustrated by it all. As he entered the front door, his eight-year-old daughter met him with a board game, asking if he had time to play with her. He said he actually felt a bit resentful because he was so tired, but knew she would not understand that. She just wanted to play a game with her dad. So he took off his coat and put a pillow under his chin while lying on the floor. They started the game. His wife came in to see about dinner and he waved her off, pointing to the board game. He had to leave again by 9 P.M. A little while later, his wife returned to try to get him to eat before leaving again. He was sound asleep, face down on the pillow. His little daughter was still playing the game with her dad right by her side. Her dad was there, although very tired. In the midst of our very complex circumstances, let us not forget the good heart of those who are trying their best to make it all work.

Then ask yourself, How can I communicate to my child that I want to spend time with him, to be there for him? There are many ways. Perhaps you could make a note to yourself to come home from work early on Wednesday and take a child out for an ice cream, just the two of you. Think of what you would write on his blackboard by doing so. Again, many of you are facing very tough personal situations. For me to suggest you do such things as in the story above may leave you frustrated and overwhelmed. Just remember, you know your own circumstances best. Do what you can—perhaps you can do an "extra effort" every other week?

Finding time will be easier if you implement and stick to regular Family Discussion Times with your spouse. Take a few minutes during that dedicated time of the week, pull out a piece of paper, and write down each child's name. Talk about each one.

USING FAMILY DISCUSSION TIME TO FULFILL FAMILY NEEDS

One of the amazing things about Family Discussion Time is that children start to recognize that parents are having them. Can you imagine what it says to a child to see his father spending some time with his mother just to think and talk about building a father-child relationship? As the child grows older and becomes more aware of the workings of the family, that child may even begin to recognize that despite Mom and Dad's busy schedules, full-time work, and life in general, his parents still take time to do things just for him.

Every time you do something for your child, whether it be

discussing ways to help him, spending more time with him, or just making yourself available for him to come to you, you leave a message on his blackboard. That message works to fulfill one of the three basic needs: feeling significant, feeling loved, and feeling competent. Your actions may lead others to write messages on his blackboard—especially if you enlist the help of brothers, sisters, friends, and extended family members. Potentially, you could fill up a child's blackboard with encouraging messages from everyone around him. Family Discussion Times and their resulting actions are powerful. They are part of a family *system* that can work. And, even if your efforts work only half the time, you will be way ahead in helping your child get what he needs in the area of basic human needs.

Let me quickly clarify what I mean by a "system." The system is the sequence parents follow in order to influence family members. By holding Family Discussion Time, parents demonstrate willingness to stop what is going on in their lives so they can think about each child and how to intentionally influence that child's life. Can you imagine the impact it might have if you taught your children about this in a Family Evening meeting? Children can tell when parents are thinking, planning, and acting on their behalf. Show them that you make your FDT plans and work to fulfill them during the week. Show them that you follow up on those plans and make adjustments as needed. FDT is like a control center for planning and action on the part of the parents.

Example 1: Tim

Let's practice the system of using Family Discussion time to fulfill the basic needs of your children. Suppose you have a son named Tim. He is eleven years old and lives in the shadow of a very successful oldest child. Tim is basically a bright and capable boy, but he gets overwhelmed at times. As you look at Tim and the "big three" needs, you rate them. You think Tim feels he is a 6 in the significant and valuable area, a 4 in the worthy-to-be-loved area, and a 3 when it comes to feeling capable and competent. Now that you've guessed—based on Tim's attitudes and actions—how he feels in each area, you have an idea of where to begin. You decide to begin with the lowest number, which relates to the need to feel capable and competent. If Tim is low on the ten-scale in the area of personal competence, it is not surprising that he is feeling down. He may not like what he sees in himself.

All a parent can really do is offer his or her best thinking and interest in a child's life and make a good-faith attempt to be helpful. You are not going to succeed at every challenge with every child. You offer what you can and then see what happens.

You now need to decide what intervention to make. You might want to discuss your ideas with your spouse or a friend—it always helps to see what others think about your own plans and theories. In what ways does Tim feel incompetent? Academically? Socially? Physically? All of these? It would probably help to evaluate each of these areas on the ten-scale. School, 5; Social, 2; Physical competence, 6. Looks like social competence could be a good place to start doing some thinking and planning to help Tim. If you are not sure about what to do to help, ask others for their advice and follow your intuition.

Let's say that during Family Discussion Time you discuss how Tim likes to do physical things, such as play baseball or other sports. You and your spouse agree that he is pretty good at physical activities. That is why you gave him a 6 on physical competence. As you and your partner talk together you begin to think that maybe you could use his physical competence to help him socially. You suggest that he invite some friends to your house to play basketball in your backyard. Afterwards, they could have a little party and watch a DVD. As a "helping" parent, you tell him that you will get the DVD he likes and buy some goodies, and he can decide who he wants to invite over. Have a talk with him about some friendly things he can do when the kids come over. That way he is doing part and you are doing part.

There is no perfect answer to any situation. Don't lose your perspective on the larger picture of what you are trying to do. That larger picture is that you are committed to doing what you can to meet your children's basic human needs.

Of course, you won't know if this will work. You may have only minimal success at first. But you are taking action. You are not waiting for something to happen in your family. Whether or not this is a perfect approach that is guaranteed to succeed is not relevant here. The *relevant* part is that you know about the three basic needs and you evaluated your child (Tim) on each one. Then you used Family Discussion Time to talk about how to help Tim in areas where help seemed to be needed. You came up with an idea and you talked it over. You talked to Tim to get some input from him, and you worked your plan. Now that it is over, you need to talk about how it went. FDT again! You might talk with Tim about how he thought it turned out, too. After all, this is about him.

You don't have to feel helpless as a parent. Do what you can do. You are not a magician. All a parent can really do is offer his or her best thinking and interest in a child's life and make a good-faith attempt to be helpful. You are not going to succeed at every challenge with every child. You offer what you can and then see what happens.

This is a pattern you can follow. If your plan needs some

modifying, then modify it and try again. Get help. Ask around. Get ideas from others who have children and see how they approached a child like this. There is no perfect answer to any situation. Don't lose your perspective on the larger picture of what you are trying to do. That larger picture is that you are committed to doing what you can to meet your children's basic human needs. It may take several attempts before you see the cumulative effect begin to pay off.

EXAMPLE 2: MICHELLE

Let's try another example. Michelle is eight. You have noticed that she is not very happy lately. You and your spouse sit down together during Family Discussion Time and evaluate her in the three key needs: significant and valuable, 4; worthy of love, 4; and capable and competent, 7. You talk together about what underlies the numbers you have used to describe her. What is going on with her? You perceive her as being "lost in the shuffle" of family busyness and complexity. She is the third of four children, the oldest being sixteen. You have two teenagers who are very busy and two younger children, ages eight and five. There is a lot going on.

Michelle is a good child and does not need a lot of attention to manage her behavior. But she seems down and sad lately. That is why you assigned the number 4 to the categories of significant and valuable and worthy of love. You assigned a 7 in competence because she handles schoolwork, chores, and dance lessons well. She is good at all of them. In the family, however, she apparently feels ignored and left out. She does not say much because she is a "good girl." What can you do?

In Family Discussion Time, you decide together that Michelle could benefit from some one-on-one time with Mom. Mom decides to ask her boss if she can leave work early every Thursday for the next few weeks. This time will be devoted to Michelle, and she can choose a fun activity to do during this time. You could go to lunch or a movie or the library or the park—anything that will allow the two of you to be together for a few hours without the interruptions of siblings or homework or chores. You also decide to ask the two teenagers in the family to do some fun activities with Michelle so that she realizes her older siblings care about her. You could choose to leave all this to chance. Maybe things will just spontaneously improve for Michelle over time. But maybe not. That is a choice parents make regularly, whether to step in or not. Sometimes it is better not to intervene. Whether you do or don't is a matter of intuition and careful consideration.

In this case, choosing to intervene will be something of a sacrifice for everyone. Family Discussion Time is the time to talk about those sacrifices and review your personal, work, and family commitments. You may look at your weekly schedule and discover that you're spending five to seven hours on a venture that you enjoy but doesn't really need that much time to fulfill properly. Perhaps you are involved in Scouting, for example, and could reduce some of your hours there for the benefit of your child who needs you. Try it for a week or two, and then at a subsequent FDT, talk about how it went and what other adjustments you might try. Parenting is a process. It takes time and some creative maneuvering. The more you talk about your children and make things work, the more you'll find that over time lots of good things can happen.

Recently, when I got up early to spend some time thinking about my family, I wondered who, on that day, needed his or her dad. That day I decided it was Debbie and Sharolyn. Debbie lives many miles away in Arizona, with her husband and four children. Because of the distance, I have less interaction with her. I wondered how I could help Debbie know she is *still* important to me (not just in general, but *to me*). I decided that I would send her a teddy bear! Keep in mind, Debbie was twenty-six years old at the time! I put a note with it that read something like, "You are *still* important to me. When you look at this teddy bear, remember that. Love, Dad."

Then there was Sharolyn. She is our youngest and was living in the East for a period of time. I also wanted her to feel that she was important to me. Her birthday was coming up, so I decided to send her a card every day for five days. On each one I wrote, "This is so you will know your dad thinks about you all the time." I think that helped her know how important she is to me. I am a very busy person, just as you are. I simply decided my taking action had to be a priority.

> *Parenting is a process. It takes time and some creative maneuvering. The more you talk about your children and make things work, the more you'll find that over time lots of good things can happen.*

SUMMARY

Time for review! What are the essential ingredients, the main building blocks of a healthy person? If you know what these are you can consider them during Family Discussion Time, where you'll ask, regarding each individual child, How do I help *this* child get the essential ingredients to help her become a whole and healthy person? I hope you will talk about your children and evaluate each one on a regular basis. Use the ten-scale to see if they are feeling fulfilled in terms of these basic human needs. In your family notebook keep track of your ten-scale evaluations to see how any given child is doing over time.

I am convinced that parents have an obligation to do things like that once they bring children into this world. I sincerely hope you are motivated by more than obligation. However, to bring children here and then declare them to be too much trouble is to back out on our original agreement and commitment to them as their parents. We must consider our parental responsibilities in life as truly sacred and be willing to give our children the best we can find within ourselves.

A Few Thoughts on Discipline

Once you understand the importance of strengthening family members and ensuring that their three basic human needs—to feel loved, valuable, and competent—are met, you'll still experience a number of parental problems. One of the big ones is discipline. Some of my clients have asked me if my concern with identifying and meeting the three basic human needs means that I do *not* support discipline. "Nice" people don't do discipline, do they? Of course they do! They must!

Children must experience logical consequences that result from their own choices, not from a parent's anger.

Discipline is an area parents struggle with from the time their children are little to the time those same children are teenagers. What is the difference between disciplining and treating children in a way that is damaging? Good discipline is important; it should be *clear* and *firm.* That means a parent sets appropriate boundaries without the accompanying negative messages discussed in the previous chapter. If it is done right, discipline can be a way of showing love and concern for the welfare of your children. Proper discipline can help you guide and teach your children how to do things, how to be responsible, how to be proper and courteous, and how to handle many other important areas of life. If you can guide your family members through the proper use of discipline, it is more likely that they will experience adequate growth and positive experiences within the three core needs.

Through discipline, your child will learn about boundaries and the consequences of his choices. Discipline is, after all, an opportunity to teach a child how to live in the family and in society. The world he lives in will discipline him if he does not learn how to follow its rules. So, lovingly but firmly, help your child, in the safety of the home and family, to experiment and learn how rules and consequences go together.

Children must experience logical consequences that result from their own choices, not from a parent's anger. Let the consequences do the work you may have previously tried to do by exerting parental power and negative emotion. This means that you should *teach* your children about the consequences of certain behaviors and choices and then *provide consequences* that predictably follow inappropriate choices made by the child. This should *not* be done with "heat and anger," but it must be done. Teach your child that behavior A leads to consequence A—with certainty. The child will then know that he can expect consequences to follow the inappropriate behavior. Guidelines and standards teach children to live competently. Developing competence is one of the three basic human needs.

If a child experiences discipline in this way, he will not feel personally demeaned. He will experience love and support, *as well as* education about how to live successfully in the family. This is a healthy combination. As a matter of fact, you have to care about a child to discipline him clearly but sensitively. As you discipline, don't lose sight of your relationship with your son or daughter.

To discipline is also to set proper boundaries, for both parents and children. Discipline should send a clear message about your expectations as a parent for good behavior in the home. It should also send a message about leadership in the home. In order to properly direct your children and teach them how to live well in their daily lives, *you* have to be in charge and sufficiently confident in your role as leader. Parents who are too passive have a hard time teaching and guiding their children. Some parents are actually afraid of their children and don't want to displease them, so they don't discipline them. Parents must be in charge, taking control when needed and giving children choices that are appropriate for them and their levels of maturity. When this happens, there is a clear feeling in the home that the parents are the leaders and, in turn, the confidants and shepherds of the family. If you refuse to take on your proper role, your children will quickly figure out that they can take charge. This is not good for you or for them. Children are not fully capable of being in charge, nor are they ready for the responsibilities that accompany such leadership. They learn to manage themselves only after you give them increasing amounts of control over their lives, *as they are ready to receive it.* This requires good judgment on your part.

Children learn to manage themselves only after you give them increasing amounts of control over their lives, as they are ready to receive it.

At the other extreme, parents should not be tight-fisted dictators. When you are disciplining, it's very important to be flexible. Some parents are overly strict and rigid in setting rules. These parents tend to follow spelled-out, unchanging rules rather than guiding principles. Healthy families tend to follow well-understood guiding principles and a few consistently implemented rules. Less healthy families have numerous rules that are rigidly adhered to; children in those families do not have enough chances to make their own decisions. Children in these families may also experience excessive punishment at the hands of their parents. Don't demand results or require behavior to achieve results. In doing so, you may unconsciously write negative and demeaning messages on your children's blackboards.

How do you know when you are being *too* strict, or you have *too* many rules, or you are *too* smothering in your parental style? When a child is under excessive duress due to living in a home atmosphere that is too "tight," parents may begin to notice that their relationship with that child is negatively affected. Children often begin to fight back and rebel, at which point the parent may want to look at how he or she is approaching that child. Some children may also begin to appear defeated and depressed. More extreme emotions on the child's part may be noted. Occasionally, some children become very compliant, but underneath their obedient exterior, they may be struggling in their unhappiness. Discipline should never involve malice or humiliation.

The overall objective of this chapter is to help you become more aware of basic human needs and how they can be addressed in the family. On a more practical basis, I hope I have helped you find more specific ways to influence your family members to be healthier people. This is a topic that needs to be revisited regularly in your Family Discussion Time, as the needs of family members change over time. Consider the following four questions about your family.

How well are your children doing on "the big three" basic human needs? _____ _____ _____ _____

_____

How well are you, as parents, doing on meeting your children's basic human needs?_____ _____ _____

_____ _____

How appropriately are you disciplining your children?_____

_____ _____ _____ _____

When you discipline, do you also strive to fulfill your children's basic human needs?_____ _____ _____

_____ _____

Chapter 8

The Supreme Importance of Family Relationships

I have a friend who has had a number of children move to foreign countries for a period of time. Each time one of them left, my friend would mail a welcome letter to his child so that the letter would be there when his son or daughter arrived! I thought that was wonderful. One day I asked him why he went to all the trouble to do that. He said, "It is very important to me that they know I am thinking of them and how much I love them at a time when they are probably feeling a bit uncertain and anxious about a new country, a new language, and a new culture. I am still their dad, even though I am a long way away."

In the more functional family, relationships are of supreme importance. They are the glue that holds the family together. Relationships deserve fervent and faithful efforts. Talk about them in Family Discussion Time. I will outline how to do that in this chapter.

Keep Relationships in Perspective

Before I delve into how to work on family relationships, it is important that I put the challenge of working on them in perspective. Relationships can be wonderful, *and* painful, *and* difficult to work with. Most families have all three types of relationships. All relationships need attention, but they must not rule your life. Sometimes you need to feel that you can step away from a relationship—especially a painful one—from time to time without feeling guilty. Remember that the goal in all things related to the family is to determine what you feel you should give or offer, and then step back. Don't try too hard to engineer results in relationships. That often produces negative results.

Working with relationships is like watering a garden. Constant watering will drown the plants. Relationships are similar. Give them attention and then back away. Let them work themselves out for a period of time. Put something into them and then wait and see how the relationship responds to your efforts. This can give you a little break too. Relationships can wear you out, so be careful not to feel too responsible for any particular relationship in your family. You should care deeply about family members, but not feel complete responsibility for them. Another person is on the other end of every relationship. That person also has a part to play in how the relationship goes.

Relationships and Meeting Basic Human Needs

In a healthy family, one reason relationships are highly valued is that they are a means by which individual worth, value, significance, and importance are communicated. It is by way of healthy relationships in the family that basic human needs can be addressed. This requires that members of the family seek to become increasingly selfless. They must get outside themselves and pay attention to each other. *We* must become more important than *me*.

Keeping in touch with each other, however, can be challenging. Most people know family relationships are important, but feel that their complex lives make relationship building difficult. One day I was walking across the university campus where I teach, wondering if I was doing well enough with a number of important family relationships. I remember thinking of the telephone slogan "reach out and touch someone."

In a healthy family, one reason relationships are highly valued is that they are a means by which individual worth, value, significance, and importance are communicated.

"That's it," I thought. "Touchpoints!" That became *my* word for what I was going to do. I did not always need to do something big or time consuming, but I *did* need to regularly reach out and touch someone in my family. *Touchpoints*. That word would represent for me any attempt I made to make *any type of contact*—big or small—with someone in the family. What I needed to do was not let a week go by without making a number of touchpoints. I have been doing it ever since, and it really helps me stay in touch. Even things like a phone call, talking briefly with family members when they come for Sunday dinner at our house, or taking one of the grandchildren for a short walk are touchpoints. Emails can be touchpoints! So many of the things recommended here can actually be fun rather than drudgery.

Contact can be meaningful even if it is short or brief, as in the case of a touchpoint. There really is no greater gift you can give a member of your family than time. I hope none of you fall prey to the old adage that lack of time can be easily offset by quality time. There is no good substitute for giving time—and as much of it as you can.

For some of you, circumstances and timing will occasionally make giving large amounts of time impossible. When that is the case, short amounts of quality time are essential. Explain to your children why large amounts of time may be hard to come by. But tell them you think about them a lot and you care greatly about them. And then support that statement by using the touchpoints concept. That will go a long way toward sustaining your relationship with each child. Any amount of time you can come up with to give as a gift of love to your family is going to help you be a better parent.

PARENTS AS RELATIONSHIP MENTORS

In the more functional family, parents nourish relationships and they teach their children how to cultivate their own relationships in the family. The parents are *relationship mentors*. Consciously and intentionally, they show their children how to make relationships a part of overall family functioning. That means parents need to try to understand relationships and how to build them. If someone in your family came to you and asked you about the essentials in creating and maintaining a good relationship with someone, what would you say?

Consciously and intentionally, parents show their children how to make relationships a part of overall family functioning.

Here are some helps:

• It's not wise just to hope that relationships will maintain themselves.

- Children want to feel important, significant, worthwhile, and loved. It is *within* a relationship in the family that children experience these feelings.
- Relationships are the delivery system for virtually all the important aspects of family life.
- Each important relationship should be considered regularly. Some of this can be done in Family Discussion Time.

You may have read that list and suddenly felt somewhat incompetent when it comes to building and understanding relationships. If so, I applaud your honesty. Part of the foundation of a good relationship is sincerity. Don't be afraid to start with sincerity and keep trying from there.

If you still feel inadequate when it comes to relationships, try picking out several people who *are* good at maintaining good relationships, and watch them for a while. Ask yourself, "What are the key things these people are doing to have good relationships?"

Write down your observations in your family project notebook so you don't forget them. If you observe several people and you keep a written record of what you notice, you can also see what they have in common.

If you are fairly courageous, you could even approach some of those people and tell them you think they do well in relationships. Then chat with them about what they try to do. You might get some great insights.

Thinking about relationships is good. But to take an *active step* and do what I just suggested is even better. *The best contributions we make to the family are almost always active.* They require that we *do* something. Now, let's go to work and see what you can do with relationships in your family. Remember, you don't have to do all relationships at once. Just give attention to one for a while and, when ready, move on to another.

FINDING OUT ABOUT RELATIONSHIPS

I suggest that you first *assess the condition* of each of the relationships you have in your family, including those with your children (whether they live with you or not), your spouse, and extended family if you want to go that far.

Sometimes, having a healthy effect on a relationship requires nothing more than touching it with some degree of interest.

Use the ten-scale to assess the condition of your relationship with each individual. This is relatively simple but extremely important. You must know where you are in order to know which relationship needs work first. Usually, when I ask parents which relationship in the family needs the most work, they intuitively know which one. Why does it need work? They know that, too. Specifically, what kind of work does it need? Ah, a great topic for Family Discussion Time! (I always find my way back to that topic because it is the centerpiece of how all this works.) Using the ten-scale to assess relationships helps parents decide where to start and what to do first.

Relationships with the littlest children require the most unconditional giving. They are somewhat more of a one-way street. I remember telling a married daughter one day when she was annoyed with her baby son, "You always love them, but you don't always like them!" She smiled knowingly.

Let's take a hypothetical example of what a parent might find by doing a ten-scale evaluation of the strength of his family relationships. Say there are five family members, as listed below. What do these evaluations tell you about this parent's relationships in our hypothetical family?

Bob: 9

Mary: 9

Tim: 3

Terry: 5

Susan: 7

What is going on with the parent and Tim? What words might describe the relationship of Tim with the parent? *Angry. Distant. Avoidant. Awkward.* Yep, that sounds like a 3. Something is really wrong with that relationship. So what is step one? How does a parent "fix" a relationship that ranks at a 3?

First, a parent shouldn't even try to fix it. That could be too discouraging. And there would be tremendous pressure to "fix" it too quickly. Relationships usually take time. Instead, a parent should decide to "contribute" to the relationship, to do something to sprinkle a few drops of water on the parched desert of that relationship. Irrigation can come later for longer-lasting effects.

What if Tim does not respond positively? He might not. The parent shouldn't expect a positive response from Tim. He can hope for one, but he shouldn't expect it. In a situation like this, it's especially important that a parent doesn't expect a positive response and make that a condition of continuing to give. Sound hard? It might be.

So, what is the real first step in a tough relationship? *Your* attitude. Oh, great, are you to blame for the relationship not being in good condition? Maybe. Maybe not. Who is to blame is not really the important question. *Who will step forward to help build the relationship is the central issue.* Who will humble himself enough to get in and help make it work? Who will say, "I will go first and contribute whatever I can to this relationship"?

Look at the example again and notice the 5 by Terry's name.

Because Tim's rating is 3, it would be easy to miss someone rated a 5, as he or she might not be in enough distress to stand out. Is there anyone like that in your family?

Attending to Relationships

Most of your relationships in the family may be in relatively good condition. Feeding and nourishing them may require only a willingness on your part to "just do it." Healthy relationships need regular attention if they are to remain healthy and not deteriorate. If you will find a time to think about the relationships in your family and specifically what you can do to nourish them (Family Discussion Time?), then you can help them be strong and vibrant. Regular relationship work, performed by you in the family, will produce an effect. It is a matter of deciding that paying attention to relationships is important. Sometimes, having a healthy effect on a relationship requires nothing more than touching it with some degree of interest. A phone call or a thoughtful note or a short chat here and there tells the other person you are thinking of her and that you care about the relationship. Some relationships are already healthy enough that that is all they need to remain in good shape. On the other hand, some relationships are hard to work with because one party (or possibly both) needs too much from the relationship. Just give it what you can reasonably give.

When it comes to attending to the relationships I have in my family, I quite often feel overwhelmed. One of the simpler things I do to "touch" an already healthy relationship is to make celebration signs. A number of years ago I decided to make such signs on special days. Here is how it works. Tomorrow might be Rodger's birthday in our family. Before I go to bed tonight, I make about half a dozen birthday celebration signs for him and put them up in the kitchen. I am sure Rodger will make it by our place pretty close to his birthday. Sherri buys me big packages of $8\frac{1}{2}$ x11-inch sheets of colored construction paper and puts them in the cupboard. I have a black magic marker, and I go to work. Some of the signs are serious, and some are funny. "Roses are red, violets are (then I pick a color and go from there)" is a *must*. That is one sign that is always in the group. For example, "Roses are red, violets are brown, we don't know what we would do without Rodger around!" Corny. Sometimes I am even more clever than that, if you can imagine. I do this for every birthday, anniversary, or special day (like a graduation, for example). It is actually fun. I love my humor. I don't know why some talk-show host has not called me.

A good friend of ours lost her young husband in a tragic accident some years ago. On the birthday following the accident, her twenty-seventh, I believe, I went to her home and put up twenty-seven signs so she would know we loved her and were thinking of her. She left them up for a week. One of our sons had a birthday, but he lived fifty miles away while he was going to law school. I made his signs and mailed them to him with instructions to please put them up in his kitchen! What is my point? Attending to relationships does not have to require major effort. You can make a truly major effort from time to time. But don't forget that most people just want to be remembered and thought of. So, try signs! They are a fun way to remember an important family relationship.

On the flip side, make sure you don't *overdo* caring for a relationship. Sometimes you can do too much and overwhelm a relationship. Always remember that in the long run, the things we are guaranteed to keep throughout life are what we learn from our daily experiences and our relationships with each other. Over my adult life I have watched many parents turn to giving their children *things* to attempt to compensate for not giving them time and interest. What your children really need is time and real interest from you. Real interest. Don't pretend to be interested—they will know when you are faking it. Struggle to gain real interest in your children, no matter how old they are.

TOUGH CHILDREN AND TOUGH RELATIONSHIPS

Almost every family has some parent-child relationships that rate high (positive) on the ten-scale and some that rate low (problematic). Some are very tough. Does that mean the family is headed by bad parents? I have asked myself that many times. I have honestly wondered if the condition of a particular child has anything to do with my condition as a parent. That is a good question to ask. Sometimes it *does* mean you have some work to do and some changes to make. But I find many parents who are too hard on themselves. Parenting and all it requires in the family is challenging work. We all come into it as beginners. We are learning how to do it while we are doing it!

So please be patient with yourself while at the same time being willing to challenge yourself to learn from other parents and get better at the job you are doing. Back to tough children. What do we do with them? I used to own a residential treatment program for seriously troubled adolescents. I saw hundreds of such youth come through our program. I was also a therapist at the Utah State Prison and worked in the Young Adult Facility there some of the time. This facility was full of younger men who had found major trouble. So I have had an opportunity to work with many teens and young adults who are in trouble. What do I say about having relationships with them? Quite often, I tell parents that their children are rejecting the parents' attempts to have a relationship. They are keeping their parents at a distance by hurting their feelings and rejecting them.

To some degree, this is what any of us could expect in a family of varied individuals. I have three suggestions. First, maintain some degree of obvious interest in the relationship with that child. Second, enlist others in the family to do the same. Make sure that the rest of the family understands that this is hard work and that it requires a faithful attempt on the part of many to "hang in there" and keep some type of relationship with the rejecting family member. You may need to settle for a less than optimal relationship. Tell the rest of the family to remember that when they get rejected. Tell them not to feel ultimately responsible for having a good relationship with that person. It might not happen for quite some time. It might not happen at all. Remember you cannot totally control the outcome of your efforts. Third, take breaks. Because you care about a relationship in the family does not mean you have to attend to it all the time. Work at it a bit and then take a break from it for a while. That is okay. We all need breaks when we are doing hard work.

Some years ago, I was working with the mother of a troubled young person. She was worn out by trying to maintain a relationship with her son. Finally, I suggested she take a break and not worry about that relationship for a while. I even suggested she spend some of the time she usually put into her relationship with him into some of the other, more fulfilling relationships in the family. She was surprised but ended up feeling very rejuvenated by that suggestion. The troubled relationship did not improve much during the time I knew her, but *she* fared better during the process of trying. Also recognize that some relationships are so damaged they may need professional help. Don't be afraid to take that route if it is needed. Connect with your family doctor or minister or other religious leader for guidance.

In my work, I see overwhelmed people and overwhelmed families who feel there is *so* much going on that they simply can't find time for each other. Our society is becoming so fast paced that you can hardly sit down for a loving conversation without your cell phone ringing. I see lonely people in families because so much is going on around the family but so *little* is going on inter-personally within the family. Cancel something and give the time to someone in your family. Pick up the phone, call that person, and say, "I just cancelled something I was going to do because I want to go to lunch with you. How about it?"

Relationships are the means by which basic human needs are often met. I am intrigued by how hard we work to fulfill the basic human needs of significance, importance, and being loved. Something drives us toward fulfilling them. We reach out with trembling hands to fulfill those needs. I guess that means they are important. Good relationships in the family go a long way toward helping family members experience satisfying levels of fulfillment of those basic human needs. When someone seeks to enhance a relationship with you, you often feel more important.

WHAT TO DO?

Nothing is more important in our lives than family relation-ships. Commit to giving something to each relationship in the family over time. As important as *what* you do is *why* you do it. Do it because you truly want to have loving and strong relationships with your family members. Success in business comes and goes. Success in school comes and goes. The same is true for hobbies and dozens of other pursuits. Inconsistencies in those areas are not so important, but we need all the consistency we can get in our family relationships. They are the lifeblood of family living. Our family relationships deserve our undying, devoted efforts. We won't be "fired" from the family or give up the "game" of family because we've gotten too old for it. Our family relationships are the most truly, deeply meaningful things we have in life. We must nourish them over and over again. We don't have to do anything really com-plicated. We just have to do something.

When you see people in your family reaching out to you, try not to hold back by clinging to old resentments or hurt feelings. Easier said than done? Sometimes. Open the door and let family members in anyway. They may want to forget the past and love you. Give them a chance.

Don't always try to do some big thing with a relationship. Just touch on it. Just offer something to it. Just give it a little. It will grow. Show the other person that the relationship has value to you. Try calling from work and saying to your seven-year-old son, "Guess what? I had a meeting this afternoon, and I just called the other people and gave them the time off. I did this because I wanted to ask if you would go with me to the swimming pool. I know how bad I look in a bathing suit, but would you go with me, and then we can get an ice cream on the way home?" What would that do for your relationship with that seven-year-old child? Or if that is "too big," call that seven-year old during the afternoon and say, "I was just thinking I wanted to talk to you!"

Quite often, relationships are significantly strengthened by a conscious choice you make to give up just one negative characteristic within the relationship.

Or what would happen if you mailed to your seventeen-year-old daughter a dinner invitation you made yourself with some funny things in it, such as, "It would be my honor, your grace, to pick you up in my horseless carriage . . . " She would never forget it. You can try it with your spouse, too. He or she might not forget it either!

Quite often, relationships are significantly strengthened by *a conscious choice* you make to give up just one negative characteristic that exists within the relationship. A common example would be a relationship that is loaded with mutual criticism. Of your own free will, you can make a conscious choice to stop injecting criticism into that relationship. Sound hard? Then start small. During the next five times you feel like being critical toward that person, reduce it by three. Am I asking you to bite your lip three out of the next five times? Pretty much, yes. Try it. *Every victory by choice makes a difference.* The other person will hopefully start to notice. She might even say something about it. Brag a little at that point. Tell her you are intentionally trying to be less critical. Such efforts within a family are inspiring. Relationships are generally not strengthened accidentally. You have to think about them. Then do something to strengthen that relationship. Maybe you should put this book down for fifteen minutes and do that. I bet there is a relationship in your family that needs you, and you need it right now.

Another characteristic of relationships in the functional family is *sacrifice.* We sacrifice for each other. Members of healthy families often give up something that they really want so that someone else in the family can have what she wants or needs. Giving up something to benefit the family or someone in the family is not so hard. All for one and one for all. Work toward thinking and feeling that way more. You certainly do need to think about yourself and how to stay healthy and happy, but I think some of us are way too "into ourselves." We need to put aside selfish attitudes and go to work for others in the family. If everyone did that, we would get more than we need!

WAYS TO INFLUENCE RELATIONSHIPS

Here are some ways you can begin to influence a relationship.

Talk

Play

Humble yourself and listen

Send notes in the mail

Go somewhere together that you both like

Treat the other person with obvious respect

Forgive

Show positive emotions

Share

Give up your ego for a day

Provide treats

Laugh

Reserve judgment

Walk together

Bowl, golf, play tennis, swim, arm wrestle, run a 5K race together

Go on a trip together

Watch him do something (let him perform in some way)

Show up at something she is going to do

Do something for him (like the dishes or polishing his shoes)

Solve a problem together

Talk about your childhood together

Go to a movie

Change your plans and offer the time saved to the other person

Become a little bit better person for her

Surprise him

Let her have her way

Send flowers

Send a gift

Send money

Send yourself (offer time and interest)

Give him some time off from family responsibilities

Watch your tone of voice

Add your own here. _____

_____

There are many more. Make a list of things you could do unilaterally to improve your relationship with someone in your family. Don't expect immediate results. It is okay to hope for changes in the relationship, but let that change go at its own pace. Just do whatever you choose out of the desire in your heart to strengthen and preserve relationships in your family. A great Family Evening activity would be to brainstorm together as a family ways to strengthen relationships. Put them on a whiteboard for all to see.

Barriers and Enhancers

Another interesting exercise that can help you strengthen and improve family relationships is to take a piece of paper and write "Barriers and Enhancers" on it. Under "Barriers," brainstorm the things you do that may create a barrier to having a good relationship with someone in your family. I recall, as a younger father, coming to the troubling realization that my temper was preventing me from having the kind of relationship I wanted in my family. It made me sick to realize how I sometimes hurt my children with my anger. I needed to make a big change. My temper was a barrier. To work on my temper I asked Sherri to signal me when I started to get too negative (before I actually lost my temper). I also told my children I was working on it (that helped me try harder because they "knew"!). Finally, when I felt myself getting too angry, I would excuse myself and walk away to try to calm down. I didn't like being angry, and I definitely did not like what it did to my children. It took me quite a while to get past it, but I finally did.

Take the time to explore aspects of your personality and family behavior that inhibit having a good relationship with a particular person in the family. Ask for advice and help on what to do. Be open and honest and humble yourself. This is a very important thing you are undertaking. You might have to change. In some circumstances, you may have to ask the person with whom you have the less-than-desirable relationship what your barriers are. I have a friend who is a meddler and entered his adult children's lives too much. He kept doing it. One day, one of them sent him a very direct email asking him to trust his children to handle their own affairs. He was stunned by the rebuke. He called me about it and asked for my advice. I said, "I suggest you accept your daughter's request and stay out of your children's business unless you see something you consider to be an emergency." He made the attempt. I think it has been hard on him! He did reduce his meddling somewhat. I think his children hoped for more. His meddling is still something of a barrier.

After you've listed the barriers, move to the enhancers, and list some things that you could invest in to enhance your relationship. Talk this over in Family Discussion Time with your partner. See if he can help you think it all through. Work out a plan for the direction you intend to take as you strengthen family relationships. Focus on what *you* do and much less on what the other family member does. Don't "give to get."

I once told a person who had a bad relationship with a family member and had been unable to improve it, "Why don't you go to that family member, tell her you want to have a better relationship with her, and ask for help?" At first he said he would be embarrassed, but then he made the venture. It had a very powerful effect, and both drew closer together in their relationship over time. It took humility for him to place less emphasis on himself, accept the potential for embarrassment, and put more emphasis on the relationship at hand. I keep mentioning *humility*. I believe that without it you can't reach some people and some people can't reach you. Without it, you can't learn some important things you may need to know about yourself.

In the more functional family, *relationships are of supreme importance.* The family should be a place where you can relax, laugh, play, enjoy, learn, survive, grow, gain wisdom, get strength, learn faith, feel support, feel important, sense your personal value and significance, feel loved, and work hand in hand. All of those things happen *within* family relationships.

Don't worry about making over an entire relationship. Start with making a small difference in it. Try keeping a journal or a notebook on your experiences. Ask your partner during Family Discussion Time to listen to you read aloud your descriptions of your efforts, successful and unsuccessful, and discuss them. There is a good chance you will get smarter about relationships. If one relationship does not respond at first, try another one for a while, and then return to the first one. This is too important to quit. Family work is the primary life work of parents. It comes before career, education, community service, hobbies, and other personal pursuits. The parents in the more functional and developing family deeply sense their obligation to do this work, and they rejoice in it. The family asks much of them, and they give it gladly and with a full heart. Sound too ideal? Do a ten-scale on "giving with a full heart." If you get 6 or below, you might want to talk it over in FDT to see what your partner thinks.

Family work is the primary life work of parents. It comes before career, education, community service, hobbies, and other personal pursuits.

Rate your relationship with each member of your family on the ten-scale (10 = strong, 0 = weak):

1. _____

2. _____

3. _____

4. _____

5. _____

Rate how you pay attention to relationships in your family in general._____

What did you learn from your self-evaluation? Which relationships need attention? During Family Discussion Time, talk about those relationships with your partner and create a tentative approach to the two relationships that need attention first. Write that approach in your family project notebook.

CHAPTER 9

The Atmosphere in Your Home

When I was growing up in Coronado, California, I always loved going to the Lewis home. Craig Lewis was a good friend, and I hung out at his house a lot. I can remember many times thinking how much I liked the actual feeling and atmosphere of his home. Since then I have tried to pin down exactly why that home affected me like it did. The home was small but extremely *comfortable*. It was not fancy or formal. It was actually quite informal, and all types of people liked to come there. Craig's parents, Howard and Ruby Lewis, were very *warm* and *accepting* people. Any time I knocked on their door, they reacted as if some big-wig had arrived. They were very *upbeat* and *positive* toward me. They displayed family pictures in prevalent places. They were humble, good people who *had time for me* and anyone else who dropped by. Their was no *pressure* or *hype* in their home. It was a nice, *gentle* place. *They* knew they were not the most important act in town, but they treated visitors as if they were VIPs.

Before you read on, go back and look at the words I've italicized in the paragraph you just read. They will help you understand the atmosphere of the Lewis home. If you wrote a paragraph like that about your home, with descriptive words in it, what would those words tell you about the atmosphere in your home?

The atmosphere of a home says a great deal about what those who live or visit there are going to experience. How does it *feel* when someone walks into your home or apartment? What is the emotional climate of your home? How each of your family members feels upon entering the doorway of your home is very important. It says something to all who enter there. The atmosphere of the home should reflect the most cherished values of the family.

Does the Atmosphere Matter?

Why does the atmosphere in the home matter? It affects how people feel, how they relate to one another, and what they think about. It also affects how basic needs are addressed. It "talks" to those in the family and hopefully nourishes and strengthens them. It can also break them down and negatively influence them. As you can see, the home atmosphere matters a great deal.

What is the ideal atmosphere in a home? Is there a certain type of atmosphere that ought to be present in the home of a more functional family? There is a range of good responses to the latter question, but I recommend that you seek an atmosphere that is inviting, comfortable, loving, helpful, and organized to communicate the most special values you hold. The things you care about should be "in the air" in your home.

Relationships in the family have a lot to do with the atmosphere in the home. Loving relationships help create a more loving atmosphere. Think of your own family experiences. When relationships are struggling, is the atmosphere in the home affected? I already know the answer you're going to give. It's impossible for the atmosphere to be *un*affected. Working on relationships helps the atmosphere, and directly working on the atmosphere also helps create a better home environment, in which relationships can become healthier.

Parents would be wise to meet with the family in Family Council and talk about the atmosphere in the home. These discussions will help members of the family understand how they can contribute to the desired feeling in the home. Holding these discussions as a family will help children come to understand that con-

The things you care about should be "in the air" in your home.

sciously promoting a healthy atmosphere in the home is something they can and should do. Involving your children in all of this teaches them how to run a family. Do this openly, and invite participation on the part of your family members. You as parents should take the lead. Here is an example of how it can happen.

As you can imagine, writing a book takes a long time. This one took me several years. During that period of time I gave various stages of the manuscript to my children to read and critique for me. Some became quite familiar with it. One day, one of my daughters who had read the manuscript was visiting our home and made some comments about what she thought Sherri and I were trying to do with our home atmosphere! I almost flipped! She talked about her own home atmosphere. My own child was thinking about the home atmosphere! She smiled when I commented on how happy it made me that she was thinking about something like that.

You too can teach your family how to promote a healthy atmosphere in the home. They can understand and do it. Since you probably don't want to write a book to accomplish this, I recommend that you discuss the characteristics of the more functional family in a series of Family Evenings. The best lessons last ten to fifteen minutes, no longer. After that, forty-five minutes of root beer. It works better with a 15:45 ratio of learning to reward. Sit your children down, identify the characteristic you're teaching, give three examples of that characteristic, ask your children to think about it and give you suggestions on how the family could incorporate that feeling into the home, then close and head for the root beer. That is success in a can!

Members of the family should be aware that their attitudes, the way they treat people, their music, indeed their "person," have an influence on the atmosphere of your home. And that atmosphere influences everyone who enters the home. Everyone has a part in it. If you have some family members who are struggling or troubled, you may find that inviting them to offer their suggestions about this and other aspects of family living helps them feel like they are an important part of your family. You could even invite their perceptions to be expressed privately if you feel they would prefer that. Even if they reject your invitation to participate, the power of the invitation may ultimately lead them into later family involvement. Sow now; reap the harvest later.

Numerous times, in an effort to determine the condition of a particular family, I have asked parents to take out a piece of paper and write on it three words that describe the atmosphere or the spirit and feeling of the family they grew up in. I then ask them to talk about it so I can get a feel for what life was like in their family of origin. I also ask them if they would like to continue to live in such an atmosphere. If not, I ask what changes they would like to make. This provides good material for discussion in their Family Discussion Time.

CHARACTERISTICS OF A PLEASANT HOME ATMOSPHERE

Let's consider some descriptions of what the family atmosphere could potentially be like. Remember that these descriptions are written in their "ideal" form. You may be some distance from that ideal. Ask yourself, "If what is written in these definitions is a 10 on the ten-scale, where am I in relation to it?"

*Inviting*_____

People want to be in this home. They are attracted to it. Once they enter this home and spend some time there, they usually want to stay or to come back again. There is some sort of magnetism to it. Visitors wish they could stay longer. Why? Maybe it was the way they were treated or the things on the wall. Maybe it was the games they played, or the hosts listening when they talked, or the smiles on everyone's faces. Maybe it was the welcome they were given or the invitation to return when they left. Perhaps it was due to the casual nature of what went on in the home—that they felt at ease, not judged or criticized. Maybe it was the humility demonstrated, the sensitivity offered, or people in the home listening a lot and talking less. Maybe it was how happy the children seemed, or that there wasn't any anger in the home, or that it was just fun to be there. Maybe it was the arm around the shoulder or the hug they had not felt anywhere else for a long time. Who knows for sure what it was, but there was something almost tangible in the atmosphere of this home. Visitors want to feel it again, and they would like to come back. The atmosphere was inviting.

*Comfortable and respectful*_____

Everyone fits in at this home. There is no push to be exactly like everyone else. There is a place for all, and everyone feels accepted by those who live in this home. Family members don't feel like they have to worry about too many things at home. There are feelings of tolerance and good will toward each other. Children feel welcome and respected, even if they don't measure up perfectly to all that might be expected of them. Visitors don't experience much awkwardness, even if they don't espouse the same beliefs as those who live there. Instead, visitors feel like they have known the family for much longer than they actually have because those who live there are anxious to include them.

There is a lack of unnecessary judgment in the air. No one is fearful about what to say or do. Everyone can be himself, and that will be acceptable. The language of the home is respectful. The parents are open and not too self-promoting. They can take feedback, even from their children, when appropriate. They ask for feedback. These parents want a solid and happy family more than they want to protect themselves. They are open to learning about how others see their family and the way it functions. Different kinds of people feel welcome here.

*Loving*_____

Everyone feels loved when in this home. They feel liked too. The spirit in this home embraces individuals warmly and makes a place for all. Children are attended to in a genuine way. Family members care for each other and for others; they open up a place for all. No one feels overly sensitive or embarrassed about himself in this home. Everyone feels valued and significant. There is a reverence for people in this home. When visitors come to this home they are treated with dignity and respect, but even the regular members of the family are considered special visitors in a certain way and are accorded a similar type of treatment. Love is expressed through patience and an absence of sarcasm. Family members feel cherished and appreciated in this home. They feel important. They count for something. They may get hugged. This family isn't in a big hurry for anyone to leave. They like having their own members and others there, and they are happy to share what they have because "you are worth it."

Family members learn to leave their critical selves outside the front door when they come in, so it feels optimistic and supportive in the home. In this family, love is offered, as much as possible, without conditions. Love is not withdrawn if the behavior of a family member is not acceptable, although family standards are clear in the family. In this family it is believed that love is too important to place conditions on. There are other things in the family that have conditions placed on them, such as use of the car, whether the children get cookies after dinner or not, or free time. But love is not one of them. It is too essential to human well-being. Keeping it in place takes hard work and lots of effort. In this home the family members try to make love a gift.

*Helpful and serving*_____

Everyone feels welcome in this home. Family members are helpful and try to give service to others. In this home, family members believe in the principle of serving others; they believe that service is ennobling and refining. Having such a belief colors all of their relationships, within the family as well as outside. Family members want to give to others and have others like it. This is not a "taking" home but a "giving" home, and all this is done with courtesy. Parents are courteous to children and to each other. Children thereby learn to be courteous to parents and to visitors. This atmosphere helps visitors feel they are more than they were when they entered, rather than less. It builds, rather than weakens. Family members feel respected and uplifted.

*Full of goodness and committed values*_____

In this home, there is a spirit of genuine goodness and a strong commitment to that which is consistent with the family's core values. Commitment to those values is easily felt, but judgment is not. This family embraces things that relate to such words as *good, right, noble, honorable,* and *moral.* This family openly acknowledges that their strength and spirit are based on their commitment to such values. They know what they stand for as a family. They are not afraid to acknowledge their commitment to the word *good.* The parents show the way by example and invite their children to seek after such clearly good things. Children are openly taught about such things as beauty, reverence for goodness, poetry, the creative handiwork of others, nature, and the noble things of life in many other forms. In this family, members like being good. In this family, good things are important and embraced. The parents teach the children about good things, and they are uplifted by what they learn. They feel a strong spirit of morality. The family talks about how their moral commitments fit into everyday life. The raw and ugly things of a pleasure-seeking society are avoided. These things are reflected in the atmosphere and spirit of their home and family.

The descriptions above are what I'd like to call thoughtful recommendations rather than requirements. They might be worth talking about it in a family meeting. Do they sound too ideal? Tough to pull off? Keep the ten-scale in mind. You don't need to do any of this at the level of 10 on a ten-scale. But maybe you could aim for 7 or higher most of the time! If you are attracted to some of the above characteristics, but feel some aspects of the definition don't suit you—feel free to alter them. My hope is that you will now think about what your home atmosphere is like and how it affects those who enter your home.

Several years ago, I taught a class at a university community education week for visiting adults. Afterward, a woman came up to me to ask me a question. She commented on what I had said about the purpose of learning about the *ideal* characteristics of the more functional family. She said that when I first used the word *ideal* it turned her off. She thought it was another "here is how to be a perfect family" talk. But she said she hung in and came to realize what I was really saying. "And what was that?" I asked her. She responded with, "The ideal is something *to aim for*. You go at it progressively, not all at once. I do not need to be 10 on the ten-scale the minute I understand the ideal. It is there to help me know where I am going on my functional family trip. It is not where I need to be today." I told her she was exactly correct and I was glad that I had not misled her. Now, let's go from principle to practice and see what we can do to bring these characteristics to life in our homes and families.

WHAT IS THE ATMOSPHERE LIKE IN YOUR HOME?

Let's see what *your* home is like. A list of possible characteristics follows that you can add to if you'd like. Please rate these on a ten-scale to give you some idea as to where your family might stand. This is quite an extensive list. Feel free to skip some characteristics and focus on others that you are interested in examining in your family. Another interesting exercise you can do with the following list is to circle the "A" (actual) or "I" (ideal) next to each item listed. The "A" is for those you believe are *actually* descriptive of the atmosphere in your home. The "I" is for the *ideal* ones that you would like to experience there. See how interesting and illuminating self-evaluation can be? Sometimes it is a little threatening, too!

Inviting   _____   A   I

Loving   _____   A   I

Comfortable   _____   A   I

Open   _____   A   I

Closed   _____   A   I

Fun   _____   A   I

Caring   _____   A   I

Tight   _____   A   I

Sensitive   _____   A   I

Overwhelming _____   A   I

Carefree   _____   A   I

Spiritual   _____   A   I

Giving   _____   A   I

Taking   _____   A   I

Generous   _____   A   I

Accepting   _____   A   I

Tolerant   _____   A   I

Rigid   _____   A   I

Fast   _____   A   I

Slow   _____   A   I

Patient   _____   A   I

Loud   _____   A   I

Rejecting   _____   A   I

Lovely   _____   A   I

Proud   _____   A   I

Friendly   _____   A   I

Relaxing   _____   A   I

Happy   _____   A   I

Hopeful   _____   A   I

Tense   _____   A   I

Mean-spirited _____   A   I

Complicated   _____   A   I

Trusting   _____   A   I

Cheerful   _____   A   I

Belittling   _____   A   I

Anxious   _____   A   I

Disorganized _____   A   I

Secure   _____   A   I

Polite   _____   A   I

Good   _____   A   I

Bad   _____   A   I

Tough   _____   A   I

Competitive   _____   A   I

Devoted   _____   A   I

Respectful   _____   A   I

Humiliating   _____   A   I

Punishing   _____   A   I

Five Key Characteristics

Now that you have evaluated this wide range of possible characteristics to describe the atmosphere of your home, talk together and see if you can identify the five major characteristics that would describe the actual atmosphere of your home. They can be positive, negative, or a mix. The essential thing is that they be honest. See if you can avoid the desire most of us have to paint a picture of our family that is too ideal. Try to make it real and accurate. If you don't know where you are, you can't plan where you want to go to work on the atmosphere of your home. To inspire your thinking, you may want to have *each* person in Family Discussion Time approach this task separately and then compare perceptions. It can be interesting and valuable to see differences as well as similarities. List the five major characteristics that currently describe the atmosphere of your family.

1.

2.

3.

4.

5.

Finally, in your own words, summarize your impression of the overall atmosphere of your home by referring to the five characteristics you listed. This is a freely written description, a final statement to help you feel confident that you have accurately described the atmosphere of your home. You could invite older children to do it too. Sometimes they experience the home atmosphere differently from the way you do.

WHERE DO YOU GO FROM HERE?

Now that you have defined the atmosphere of your home, how satisfied are you with it? What changes would you like to make? How do you intend to go about it? It is time to make some decisions and then take action. This last segment of the chapter is properly concluded when you have written down a specific description of what you are going to do to produce an atmosphere that is the kind you want to have in your home.

The atmosphere of your home is the soil in which each family member grows and finds vital nourishment.

The atmosphere of your home is the soil in which each family member grows and finds vital nourishment. My goal is to help families know where they are so they can determine more clearly where they would like to be and then define the steps they must take to get there. Rather than wishful thinking, let's work with a concrete plan.

THE PLAN

Take a piece of paper (or maybe even your family notebook), and write a general description of how you want the atmosphere in your home to improve. Remember, you are seeking improvement, not perfection.

Next, choose as many as five *specific* aspects of your home atmosphere that you want to enhance. If that is too much for you, choose just one to work on.

1.

2.

3.

4.

5.

Finally, make a list of *specific* things you can do to improve your home's atmosphere in the areas you have just selected. This is the challenging part of the plan—actually doing something. The plan usually bogs down here. Please don't let that happen because this is where changes begin to happen. This is where progress and improvement can actually occur in how your family functions. List the specific actions and decisions you will make to bring about the overall improvement you described.

1.

2.

3.

4.

5.

How Do You Feel Now?

So, how do you feel? You have done some good thinking and some important planning. You have reminded yourself and your spouse (you're having those FDTs, right?) of the improvement you are seeking and have also chosen one of the specifics you listed above and decided *what, who, when,* and *how* it will happen. Those specifics are essential, allowing you to follow up at the next Family Discussion Time to see how things went and what adjustments you might need to make to help things work a little better. This overall plan allows you to actually do something to help your family move in your personally chosen, desired direction. Whatever hard work and sacrifice you make here for your family is worth it. You are being given lots of suggestions—remember that whatever your personal circumstances are, you can do as many or as few of them as seems sensible and appropriate for you to try out. I am not trying to kill you off but rather to offer encouragement.

Using the ten-scale, rate the overall quality of the atmosphere in your own family and home._____

CHAPTER 10

Teaching the Important Things

Ihave a friend who has done some very inspiring things in terms of teaching in the home. Every night before he goes to bed, by self-appointment, he puts a 5x7-inch card on the refrigerator with a new word on it for the family to talk about at breakfast the next morning. For example, he might put up *discrimination*. That's it. He just posts the word. At the breakfast table the next morning someone either guesses what it means or looks it up in the dictionary. Then they talk about how it could potentially be used. I've noticed that his children generally do well in school and seem to like learning. Efforts such as these certainly communicate how much this parent values learning. His children, undoubtedly to varying degrees, have seemed to pick up the same zeal for learning.

Think of half a dozen families you know. Do the parents teach in the home, actually teach with their children as "students"?

Or is family learning something that just happens by chance? Is teaching in these homes done informally or formally?

Teaching and learning are typically associated with experience in schools. Do you ever think of the family as a school? If I were to ask you, "What is the most important school your children attend?" How would you answer? Would you say, "Their public or private school, of course"? Those who choose home school for the formal education of their children would likely come closest to the answer I am going to propose simply because they accomplish the education of their children at home. *The most important school your children attend is the family school.* In the more functional family, teaching is important. The healthy development of individuals has much to do with their participation in learning.

USING FAMILY COUNCILS TO LIVE AND LEARN TOGETHER

The functional family is a school where imperfect people live and learn together. That members of a functional family are imperfect is significant because, as long as individuals are imperfect and know and acknowledge it, they can still grow. Imperfect people need help, examples, and mentoring. In the more functional family, members can get those things. After all, the functional family is never really finished; it is always a work in progress. If a family weathers many storms together, they likewise *learn* a lot by being refined and schooled *together.* In the more functional family there is less fear of imperfection because members are able to deal with imperfections together. They are able to *endure* together.

The idea of family endurance is important. It is crucial that you discuss family endurance together and define what it means. I propose it means that family members agree to go the distance together regardless of the difficulties and challenges they face. It means that you are committed to each other and don't quit when the going gets tough. Discuss this in a Family Council. Some characteristics of the more functional family need to be absolute. This one needs to be as absolute as you can possibly make it. In everyday terms, your family needs to have a plan for how you'll all hang in there together. Invite family members to share examples of how the family has endured together. Discuss what it took to do so.

The functional family is a school where imperfect people live and learn together.

Family Councils and Family Evenings are great settings for helping each other learn and grow. One of the memorable Family Councils held in our family occurred many years ago when one of our younger sons was in the early years of grade school and was having difficulty learning to read. We held a Family Council with the older children to get their input on how we could help him. I will never forget how our older twin girls enthusiastically offered to help him improve his reading.

"What could you do?" I asked.

"We could read with him every day after school," they chimed in.

I explained that was part of his problem—he couldn't read very well. So I suggested that Sherri and I make some vocabulary word cards for them to use with him. They could just review the flash cards with him several days a week after school. Over a period of many weeks they did just that. They helped him immensely in improving his reading. Over the years I have reminded the two older siblings of what they did for their younger brother. It helped him, but it also helped *them* feel good about themselves in our family. It helped them feel significant, which is a basic human need. Family Councils are wonderful in providing the opportunity to sit down together and take a shot at solving a problem that affects a family member or the family in general.

By participating in such councils, family members are also being taught how to run a family. They see that the family has a sensible direction to it. They clearly see the parents leading this effort. They see that it's not necessary to know everything; the combined creative thinking of family members can elicit great ideas. In Family Councils, ask your children what they need help with. Or give them some topics you feel are important to consider and then ask them which ones they feel are most important. Let them do some teaching on these topics. This will keep them involved in the family learning process, rather than having all the teaching come from you. If they feel vested in the family and the family process, then they will feel it is *their* family as well as yours. With lots of help and input, your job as parents is to give thought to what the family needs to learn and then go about the vital work of teaching your children and showing them how to live. It is a very conscious effort.

FIND A MENTOR

Remember that parents are learners too. We all need help, even parents. I strongly recommend that every parent should have his or her own parenting mentor. From that mentor you can learn new ideas, skills, and abilities to help you be a more effective parent. Who could you use as your parenting mentor? These would be parents you know and in whom you have a strong sense of confidence because you have noticed their good parenting skills. They have a good sense of direction and commitment in their parenting; and you could go to them for help and tutoring no matter how far down the parenting road you have traveled yourself. At some point, perhaps you can serve as a parenting mentor to other parents who are looking for help. I love the word *mentoring* as it applies to the family. Webster defines a mentor as a "trusted counselor or teacher, or loyal advisor." Observe carefully those you choose as your parenting mentors. Select specific areas of parenting to work on. Then watch your parenting mentors. See how they do it. Also, make a list of questions about your own parenting that you would like to explore and talk over with your parenting mentors. The ideas you obtain would make great planning material for a Family Discussion Time.

PARENTS ARE TEACHERS

Parents must be teachers in the home. Many parents know this is important, but they get so caught up in the busyness of everyday living that an attempt to consciously teach their children just does not appear on the daily agenda. The complexity of daily life in the family can make direct contact in the form of teaching very difficult to accomplish, something that is easy to put off until later. But later may never come.

Many parents also worry about getting a negative response from their children when they attempt to sit them down and teach them. Don't let the difficulty prevent you from trying. What follows are some suggestions to get you started in your teaching role, as well as some explanations about different types and styles of teaching.

HOLD REGULAR FAMILY EVENINGS

One suggestion is to have a Family Council to casually discuss how it would benefit everyone in the family if you sat down together and had short lessons or discussions on topics of value to the family. Suggest that these discussions or lessons become part of the Family Evening. Once you have introduced the principle of *learning together*, it may be easier to actually hold additional family meetings later. In my experience, children are drawn to family learning activities when they see those activities are important to a parent. I recommend that you actually talk about that by saying something like, "I really want us to learn important things together. Your mother and I would like you to know how we feel about certain things. We wish our parents had taken the time to teach us when we were young. I hope you will work with us and help us by participating. We will do our best." Children will sense your sincerity.

PRACTICE DIRECT AND INDIRECT TEACHING

It is important that your family members, over time, come to *expect* to be taught by their parents. There are two types of family teaching: direct and indirect. *Direct teaching* means you sit your family members down in a setting such as Family Evening and talk with them. You briefly present a topic, and everyone who is interested gets a chance to discuss it. *Indirect teaching* is when something else does the talking for you. Indirect teaching is more informal and somewhat less intense. Some personalities prefer the indirect approach to family learning. For some, taking the intensity out of teaching in the family is the best way to do it. An example of indirect teaching would be to put up a picture or a quote on the refrigerator. You don't sit the family down and teach them, but you put up something they will see and perhaps think about. Indirect teaching can stand by itself or be a support to direct teaching. For example, let's say you have a family learning experience on the importance of having a healthy body. You then put up on the family bulletin board, over the next week, daily quotations or information that has something to do with the family discussion you had together. Each time the children see the quotation for the day, they might flash back to the lesson you taught on that topic. That is one way to combine direct and indirect teaching.

Most parents do very little direct teaching in the family. But doing it to any degree can have a significant impact on the development of family members. That is why Family Evening can become so valuable. It can be time for family fun and togetherness, *as well as family teaching*. I am often asked what possible topics parents could teach! Wow. The list is infinite, as you can imagine. (Later in this chapter you'll learn more about important things a parent could teach). You can teach *anything* that seems important to teach in your family. You can ask your children for suggestions. "We will have a brief lesson at each Family Evening—what are you interested in learning about?" Also ask, "After we learn together, what would be a good reward for all of us to enjoy?"

Just for purposes of illustration, you could teach on topics such as certain verses from your own religious literature, courtesy, how to make a decision, how to read effectively, colors (for little ones), study skills, developing mutual respect for each other in the family, time management, handling anger, exercise, dealing with depression, relationships with grandparents, and so on. See how interesting it can be? But keep your lessons brief! Fifteen-minute lessons are the best.

And don't make teaching too complicated. Any time you stop the normal routine of family life and take just a few minutes to talk together and learn about a subject of significance, you offer something important, given in love, to your family. Sometimes you will do it formally in a small group, or one on one. But more often than not, it will be done casually and informally. Just the fact that you are thinking about your role as a teacher in the family will begin to pay off. Your children will usually notice. And what are they learning? Parents are teachers. And your children are getting a great message on their blackboard: "I am important enough for my parents to stop what they are doing, take some time to think about me, and teach me something useful." What a powerful message.

When our children were growing up, we had a family tradition called Study Time. Each school night after dinner, the TV was turned off, no one went out to play, other activities were curtailed, and we designated one hour for study time. Everyone knew that hour was for homework or for other learning if someone had no homework. Some had work that took more than an hour, so they studied before or after Study Time as well. But we had at least one designated hour, with no competition from other family or personal pursuits, in which everyone could study and learn. This not only helped our children do better in school but also helped communicate to the children the value of education and learning. We had a family meeting and talked about Study Time, its purpose, and why *we* thought it was important. Then we did it regularly. We were not perfect at it—with ten children we were not perfect at anything—but we held Study Time with a good degree of regularity, and our children caught on to it as a tradition that paid dividends over time. They still talk about it today, years later. One of them, now in his thirties, told me, "Because of Study Time, we all knew how much you valued learning in our family."

We have some neighbors who instituted a very simple family learning tradition that was a part of dinnertime. They would join at the dinner table and, as they began to eat, they would ask if anyone had a recent "learning experience" to share briefly. There was a moderate expectation that someone would have something to share. Sometimes even more than one learning experience was shared. The father of the family told me that one of the most powerful of these "dinnertime learning experiences" came when his ten-year-old daughter said that she had a bad time at school and no one would play with her. She said she realized that she would soon be home where she was loved. She had learned something very important about her family and she shared it. What a great tradition.

Have Fun

Try to make some of these direct or indirect learning topics just plain fun and interesting. You could, for example, teach your children how to cook, how to paint, how to hit a golf ball, or how to work cooperatively in building a human tower! You could even have as your topic how to tell a good joke!

Teaching almost anything will eventually pay off, because the family sits down together and has a joint learning experience.

What you teach is important. But *the very fact that you teach* is more important. When you can, take a fun approach to teaching and learning. Teaching almost anything will eventually pay off, because the family sits down together and has a joint learning experience. Taking time to prepare for teaching and thinking about your children shows you care about them. That is the underlying message to your family. Some will recognize that immediately and appreciate it. Others may take some time. Still others may never see what you did, but the odds are in your favor over time. I believe such efforts really pay off. How good you are at it is not as important as that you cared enough to try.

Teach through Example

Another critical form of family education comes by way of your example. I ask myself routinely if I can recommend my life to my children for emulation. Would I feel comfortable asking my children to live in accordance with my public *and* inner, private life? I am convinced that for the sake of one's children, each parent must be willing to do a thorough self-evaluation in both the public and the private areas of their lives. We live in a world in which we allow the public self to be quite different from the private self. Unfortunately, personal integrity does not seem to be as valued as it used to be. Are we willing to challenge ourselves and require that our public and private lives have more consistency and integrity, if not for our own well-being then for our children? Will you place all aspects of your public and personal life on the family altar?

If you can't recommend yourself completely and entirely to your children, then what do you need to change about yourself?

I know my private self. I may think it is *totally* private. And yet to a certain degree, it shows outwardly. It is a part of me. Even though I can try to hide it from view, I really can't hide it completely. My private self is part of the fiber that makes me who I am; it affects my words and actions in both obvious and subtle ways. We won't long fool our children about who we are at the core, especially as they get older.

Children have an uncanny sense about their parents. That means we must do some deep and honest introspection. Who am I really? If someone followed me around for a week and took notes on all he observed about me, and then wrote down a list of what he thinks I value, what would he say about me? That might be worth taking a few minutes to ponder. Take out a piece of paper and write down a list of the things you believe you value. Is there evidence to support that you really value those things? I have always liked the concept of *core values*. They are the guiding values of your life, which you personally have chosen through a thoughtful process. It is fascinating to actually list what you think you value and then talk about what you have come up with while in Family Discussion Time. To share them in Family Evening with your children can be a great experience too.

I once worked with a couple in marriage counseling when the issue of internal consistency and integrity came up. They each felt the other was publicly one thing and privately another. I asked them if they would accept a challenge from me. I invited them each to choose one person they trusted and have that person write down what he or she felt were the most important things in each spouse's life. What an eye opener! Both were somewhat surprised to find that an external, impartial observer did not find evidence to support a number of the values they felt they had, at least not to the degree that they felt they possessed them. They said they valued certain things, but the evidence to back up some of those values was not very strong. After reviewing the observers' opinions, they agreed that they both lacked a certain amount of internal consistency on personal values. And their children were watching and imitating. Your children will do the same to you. Our examples, good or bad, communicate and teach very powerfully.

Here is a parental challenge for you: Ask yourself if you would be willing to invite your children into your inner life and recommend that they try to be like you in every way. If not, why not? The answer may give you an agenda for change. If you can't recommend yourself completely and entirely to your children, then what do you need to change about yourself? If every parent would ask himself this, we likely would have much better parental examples for our children to follow. Isn't that teaching? Your *example* is one of the most powerful forms of teaching you can offer your children. "Be like me." How many can say that in full honesty? You don't need to be perfect, just honest. There is nothing wrong with showing your children an imperfect example, as long as it is an honest one. This says to your children, "I am in good shape in some ways and not so good in others, but I am working on it because I want to show you a better example. The best way I can help you in your life is to show you an honest parent who is working at providing you with an improving example to follow." That is ideal but also very healthy; it does not make you be perfect, but it does require some gut-level honesty on your part. *What if your children were just like you?*

REMEMBER WHY YOU ARE TEACHING

Some parents try to get out of teaching by saying someone at school or a youth program is doing it. No! Don't let anyone else take that responsibility away from you! You are the parents, which means you are also the *family teachers*. There are no more important teachers in the family than the parents. If there are two parents in the family, don't let one parent be the teacher while the other simply supports such a venture. One may enjoy it more, taking the lead, but the other should also see the value of it and give it a try. Both parents need to teach and model important things.

If you are by yourself in this parenting venture, you might attend activities with another family. Some people tell me single parents are too busy to do joint ventures with other single parents. That may be true for you. But if you can, try it out from time to time. If you have some older and some younger children, then get the older children involved in the planning and implementation. Let them help you, so they can have the opportunity to experience the fulfillment of helping the family. You can put a great message on their personal blackboard if you take a moment to say something like, "Thank you for working with me on trying to teach the younger ones. Your example is so important and the love you are showing by working with them is wonderful." Do you think that would help a child feel significant and important?

TEACHING EXPECTATIONS

You also should have reasonable expectations about what happens when you teach your children. Many lessons that you teach today will not be learned until later. Don't go into Family Evening with the expectation that you will sit them all down with big smiles on their faces because they are so full of anticipation. And definitely don't expect that they will beg for a one-hour lesson with a quiz at the end to show you how much they learned from your great teaching! What should you expect? Don't have unreasonably high expectations; just give it a try. In my observations of the family, I have found quite often that children who were directly taught by their parents remembered those experiences later in their lives. They did not always remember all of the specifics taught but they treasured the loving and caring spirit that led their parents to teach them. They also fondly recall that their parents finally learned that the best lesson was one that was *short!* Succinctly make your teaching point, parents, and then spend lots of time playing and having fun. The expectation of fun and treats after a short lesson increases the children's willingness to endure your "little" lessons. Are you buying them off? Maybe!

Take this aspect of parenting very seriously and plan what you want to teach your children (use Family Discussion Time to plan—you knew that I would mention it again). Then teach it to them and remember that how they react or what they do with what you taught them is not entirely within your span of control. Try not to be overly concerned about that. Your major concern should be that making the effort to teach is very important in the more functional family.

How often have you heard an adult say, "My parents taught me the importance of hard work and I sneered and resented it then, but now I am sure glad they taught it to me"? As anyone who has ever done much teaching knows, sometimes students don't accept the things we teach, at least not in the moment they are taught. We teach and set an example because our children need us to show them how to live responsibly and effectively. We do not teach because we know our efforts will be successful. We teach because it is our responsibility to teach our children. Remember, it is what we offer that is most important. Then we hope that our teaching will produce the desired results, knowing that, in some cases, it might not.

WHAT AND HOW TO TEACH

Some parents worry about their teaching abilities. Please don't worry too much about how good you are at teaching. Don't merely hope to succeed either. Having a good experience in teaching your children has several important components to it. Planning must happen first. Family Discussion Time is a good opportunity to take out a sheet of paper and write the answer to the question, "What are the five most important things I need to teach my children in the next few months?" These could be general items for the family to learn together, or some specific lessons designed for one of your children in particular. Just brainstorm, and ask your partner to do the same.

"What are the five most important things I need to teach my children in the next few months?"

Because I challenged you to come up with the five most important things to teach in your family—and because I don't want to leave you wondering about what could be considered important—I asked my ten adult children what they could recommend as you make your list. Their recommendations follow (not necessarily in order of priority):

- Specifically teach about how important relationships are and how to strengthen them. Know what is going on in each other's lives.
- Teach about fun, how it bonds you together and lets you have time together.
- Teach the importance of being strong in your convictions and how to make good decisions in the face of peer pressure.

- Teach the importance of good communication and trust in the family.
- Teach about the importance of education. Read together and teach your children to love learning. Learn *with* your children. Make learning fun.
- Teach how important *each* individual is in the family. Help each one know he or she is wanted, needed, loved, and appreciated. Support family members in developing their own talents and abilities.
- Teach children how to serve others.
- Teach about spirituality and faith.
- Teach family members the importance of hard work and effort.
- Teach about integrity, respect, humility, and gratitude.
- Teach children how to make decisions and solve problems.
- Teach endurance in facing problems.

More than half of those suggestions were made by two or more children in my family. All came from them in their own words. You might notice that my consulting my children on this question is an illustration of getting your family together to have a Family Council to discuss important things.

List the five things you feel you currently need to teach your children. See what your partner thinks. Do it independent of each other at first and then share your thinking.

1.

2.

3.

4.

5.

Make a final list together of things that you conclude are important to teach your children right now. Really talk it over. Think of specific children in terms of who needs to learn what. You may want to teach on personal topics, how to be healthy, how to solve a problem or make a decision, how to develop mutual respect in the family, how to have more interpersonal courtesy, how to develop better study habits, how to bowl, how to have more fun as a family, how to manage money, or how to choose a career. There are many potential topics. Some will require you to do some personal study yourself. Your children will be impressed that you were willing to do that for them. If you have not done family teaching before, you'll discover a natural high that comes with doing it. Some of these things might also be better taught during situations or "moments" in which the principle involved is practiced. Watch for "teaching moments" in your daily activities, especially during especially difficult or troubling times. There are a lot of lessons that can be taught in times of struggle.

If you have an actual lesson during Family Evening, remember to keep your teaching time short. These lessons are best learned if you keep them to about ten to fifteen minutes. At times invite one or more of the children to help you teach. In some cases, you can have them teach a brief segment of the lesson or share their opinion, depending on their age. Teach them something and give them a chance to talk it over a bit. Get lots of root beer and ice cream for afterwards or make a promise to play a favorite game or visit a favorite location. Kids learn faster when they get a treat or have fun. Parents do too!

Then look for ways during the following week to casually bring up one-on-one with some of the children whatever you talked about in your Family Evening lesson. Make these exchanges intentionally very brief. You can see that teaching your family is not extremely complicated or time consuming, but it does require your interest and attention. You have to come up with the lesson topic, provide some brief teaching on the topic, have a reward for listening, and then make some effort to follow up one on one. Over time two things will probably happen: (1) Your children might actually learn some things, and (2) they will start to notice that parents teach. The secondary lesson inherent in any lesson you teach in the family is that your children are learning how to teach and run a family.

Most important is that you gather your family around you regularly. Let them hear your teaching voice and feel your love as you reach out to them. In all that, have fun.

What is most important is that you gather your family around you regularly. Let them hear your *teaching voice* and feel your love as you reach out to them. In all that, have fun. Celebrate and participate in all the good things a family can be. Have family meetings together, like Family Evening and Family Councils. Make decisions *together*, discuss important topics *together*, and eat ice cream *together*.

Another great way to learn in the family is through email. You can even designate one day a month in which you send out a family learning topic on email to all family members who have their own email address. All ten of my children have their own email addresses, so I send quotations, ideas, and experiences to them regularly (much to their chagrin sometimes, I might add). I invite them to share things they learn with the family or to share experiences in which they have learned something significant. You can even set up a family website, where family members can post new things they have learned or experiences they have had from which the whole family might benefit.

A FAMILY ATTITUDE LEADS TO FAMILY LEARNING

No matter how or what you teach, doing so will help nurture a family attitude. A family attitude involves moms and dads, sisters and brothers, who think about each other and want to share things with each other because they care about each other.

Let's look at an example. You feel that raising responsible children is important. So during Family Discussion Time, you plan a Family Evening lesson on responsibilities in the home, including all the things that need to be taken care of for a home to run smoothly. You make a list of who will do what, and plan to talk those over with the children. You plan to teach and discuss this at the next Family Evening, which you hold once a week. You decide whether one or both of you will teach it and plan some additional indirect teaching ideas for later in the week. You decide who will make a work chart that lists the responsibilities of each family member.

Or your family might prefer to have the family talk together about what is needed and why it is important. The children could brainstorm all the things that need to be taken care of in the home and family. You could actually make a family work chart right there on the spot! If you did this, you could then ceremoniously march into the kitchen and post it on the bulletin board! Every time the children saw the family work chart, they would be reminded of the family topic you tackled together and the family discussion that followed. As parents, you planned it, taught it, discussed it, built it, and posted it! And you involved other family members because you know that when children help in the process they feel like this plan is theirs as well as yours. This is family involvement and learning at its best. Do you see what this is all about? A family is working together and doing something for their own good! That is wonderful. We must do all we can to promote such responsibility in the family.

Afterwards you can have treats or watch a DVD! Someone can be in charge of ice cream and cookies to celebrate all you've accomplished. While you are eating, one of the parents can say, "Isn't this great? We all learned something together and we did it as a family. I love it!" This same process can be applied to learning how to cook, how to succeed in school, how to sew, or how to speak Spanish.

Parents teach, children learn. Try the reverse sometimes: Children teach, parents learn. It is wonderful to see family members come together and mutually benefit. This routine has the potential to produce some wonderful family learning and bonding over time. At first it takes some adjustment on the part of parents and children. Stay with it. It is worth it.

THE PARENTAL TEACHING FORMULA

Here, then, is what I call the *parental teaching formula:* Join together in a Family Evening and teach your children. That is direct teaching. Then put things around your home that will reinforce what you have taught without saying much additionally. That is indirect teaching. Finally, openly practice in your own daily lives the things you want your children to do and become. That is teaching by example. That is a teaching package that will give your children a home learning environment that will stimulate them in many different ways.

Spontaneous teaching moments will also happen. Keep in mind specific things you would like to teach a specific child, and then look for opportunities to teach during brief moments of opportunity that just pop up now and then. For example, you are on your way to the store to get some groceries. Suddenly it hits you: Take Emma with you! It could be a potential teaching moment. You can have thirteen-year-old Emma all to yourself for a half hour. You invite her to go and she says yes, especially after you promise her a treat on the way home. You have been thinking about her and you know she is starting junior high the next week. She seems a little down, and quite worried.

So, what could you teach Emma that would help her? There are many answers to that question. The crucial point is that you are *thinking about Emma.* You are looking for opportunities to help and guide her. You have a chance now. You can ask about how it feels to start junior high and do some listening. Possibly the right moment will present itself where you can share some of your own experiences of feeling anxious about a new school year, and perhaps how to handle it. Be careful not to just jump in and talk about yourself, or you may forget Emma is there! Just be personal, loving, and brief!

In your Family Discussion Time each week, it may be wise to keep track in written form of the topics you decide to teach about in the family. From time to time you can go back over the record. Over months of time you will be amazed at all the things you talked about and how hard you worked at family matters, children, and other family issues. If you ever get discouraged about your parenting, go back and look at the record of how hard you have thought, planned, and loved. Remember, all you can really do is offer that to your family. You will see that you really did offer a lot. Good for you. As a part of all that, you can look at your specific teaching efforts in the family and ask each other how many you feel actually had a positive impact. If you notice some that did, you can celebrate! You are accepting your teaching responsibility as a parent and you are working on it.

Rate yourself as a parent in the area of teaching._____

What are the next steps you need to take to act as a family teacher?

CHAPTER 11

Staying in Touch with Home and Family

I know a family in which the father took responsibility for back-to-school nights and all parent-teacher conferences during the school year. I talked with him about it once and asked him why he had chosen to accept that responsibility, because things like that have traditionally been done by the mother. He said, "I like it. It is not my wife's favorite. There are other things in our family life she enjoys doing more. So, I took that one. And I feel more 'in the know' when I am there each time to make sure there is proper communication between us and our children's teachers. Later my wife and I talk about what I find out."

I wondered if they had thought out other aspects regarding division of labor in the family so well. I could tell they were communicating about it and they seemed to have a good sense of who was responsible for what in the family. That was good.

In more functional families, there are clearly defined roles and responsibilities for each parent and child. Family members know and fulfill their roles and responsibilities. They often determine what these roles are in a family meeting. The parents take the lead in making sure there is a clearly determined *organization* within the family.

Parents are family mentors, aware of how important it is to show their children how to do things. They model for the children. They hold Family Evening or Family Council for two reasons: (1) so that children have practical experience within the family and can see the actual results of family discussion; (2) so that children begin to understand how important such family interactions are; they actually learn how to hold and conduct family meetings.

Someone Needs to Be in Charge

Do you believe that there are a certain number of very important aspects of family life that must be taken care of with certainty? I'm guessing that your answer is yes—with an exclamation point at the end of your statement! In my years as a marriage counselor I have met many, many couples whose marriages were in trouble because their marital and family responsibilities were set up in an unsatisfactory way. Daily life, full of so many important things, was unpredictable and chaotic.

Most people expect that those things which are important to them will be taken care of. I am talking about the key elements of daily family living. Who is responsible for making sure these key elements happen? For daily life to have some predictability and organization to it, someone should be *primarily* in charge of each of the key aspects of family living. Some form of defined family organization is important. Take that up in Family Discussion

Time and see what you feel comfortable with. There are no right or wrong answers, but there is a need for clear organization and well-defined assumption of responsibilities by parent-leaders.

Roles and responsibilities cover virtually anything that goes on in the family. Every major family issue or need should have

Changes in family life are the only things that are constant, which means that changes in responsibilities should be expected and accepted.

someone in charge of it, someone who feels responsible for it. Parents should not just hope that things will be taken care of. One parent should say, "I will be responsible for that area. I am committed to it." What should the other parent do in that area? Whatever the two of you agree on. If it is the best approach for you, you can decide to back up each other up in each area. One of you can be *primary* supervisor of a particular aspect of family living, and the other can automatically be *secondary*.

You might, however, feel like this system doesn't work in all areas. So you may decide to use the primary/secondary approach in some areas, but let one person take over completely, calling for help when needed, in other areas. Sometimes you may agree to just split a certain responsibility fifty-fifty. Be careful if you choose that course; sometimes that ends up communicating that no one is really responsible for the area, and then no one does much with it.

None of this is permanently set in concrete. During any Family Discussion Time you can decide to revisit any and all responsibilities and rearrange things if they are not working well. Changes in family life are the only things that are constant, which means that changes in responsibilities should be expected and accepted. This is why a regular Family Discussion Time each week is so helpful—it's a time to talk, evaluate, and reconsider what needs to happen in the family.

Some areas of family living that need attention can be very

broad (like nurturing and giving love) or as specific as you want them to be (like helping a handicapped child get dressed every day). Every important family responsibility belongs to one of the parents unless you agree to handle a few areas otherwise. The children should also have family responsibilities. They must learn how a family works and how important a family is by working to benefit the family. Generally, however, don't give children *final* responsibility; they should work under one of the parents. There should always be a parent-leader. This demonstrates the principle that parents are ultimately responsible for what goes on in the family. Children can have major responsibilities, but not final responsibility. As an example, one parent may be responsible for yard work, while a child may have a specific responsibility to weed the garden weekly under the direction of one of the parents.

As the parents make decisions on who will shepherd which family responsibilities, it is crucial that final decisions be mutually agreed upon. Talk about it, debate it, talk about it some more, but the agreement ultimately works best if it is mutually agreed upon. Don't accept your responsibility bitterly! Know what is expected of you as a parent and accept it fully and completely. This is very important.

HOW TO IDENTIFY IMPORTANT FAMILY ROLES AND RESPONSIBILITIES

In this week's Family Discussion Time your topic could be family roles and responsibilities. What is your task? First, you need to define key roles and responsibilities that help your family function as you want it to. Together, take out a piece of paper and write roles and responsibilities at the top. Just brainstorm every-thing important that comes to your mind in this important area

of family living. Let's look at some possibilities that might appear
on your list:

> Who will earn the money to support the family?
> Who will teach the children?
> Who will keep the house organized and clean?
> Who will cook?
> Who will nurture the children?
> Who will make sure Family Evening or Family
>   Councils happen?
> Who will help with homework?
> Who will read with the children?
> Who will do the yard work?
> Who will do the dishes?
> Who will fix things?
> Who will see that children's activities are properly
>   supported?
> Who will follow up with teachers at school?
> Who will help the family have fun together?
> Who will make sure Family Discussion Time hap-
>   pens weekly?
> Who will be in charge of special needs that children
>   may have?

Having made your own list, similar to the example above,
the next step is to identify *which* of the key roles and responsibilities on the list will go to the father and which to the mother.
This will require some discussion. Keep in mind the personal
situation of each parent. Try not to overload either partner. And
remember, all areas of family responsibility are not of equal
importance. Some parents may be so busy that some items on
the list can go temporarily unassigned or be assigned to older
children. Once it appears on your personal list, however, *you are*

the responsible person in that area of family life. This is a particularly sensitive area for single parents, who will look at the list of
examples above and say, "Good grief! I have *all* the items on *my*
list!" There is no question this dilemma is one of the supremely
difficult parts of single parenting. The list is too long without
someone to help. My suggestion is that you enlist the help of
older children on some of the responsibilities. If you are fortunate enough to have extended family members who can assist in
some areas, ask for help. Beyond that, you have to shorten your
list to include only *essentials* and leave some things for another
day when you can get to them. That is undoubtedly easier said
than done.

DEFINE THEM—COMMIT TO THEM

The most important thing about roles and responsibilities is
that you *define* them, agree on who does what, and make a commitment to shoulder your responsibilities faithfully, whatever
they are. In some cases, you may need to take upon yourself
something you really don't want to do. Do it for a while and
then, during Family Discussion Time, seek relief and trade for
another family responsibility. Share how you feel about your various roles and responsibilities. To be "heard" almost always
makes a person feel better. But be clear on who is responsible for
what. When someone is clearly in charge of essential family
responsibilities, a comfortable, nice structure to family living will
present itself. Manage your responsibilities as happily as you can.
Take pride in the notion that you are *intentionally* doing something for your children and your family that will make them
happier and make home life more pleasant, even if you have to
sacrifice or lose some sleep in the process. That is what parenting is all about.

Again—Conscious and Intentional Parenting

Taking on roles in the family is, in every sense of the idea, conscious and intentional parenting. It shows that what you are doing as a parent is well thought out and that you have made a commitment to your role. It also requires that parents be *present*. You can't be off the premises if you are going to assume some primary responsibility in the family and successfully follow through on it. You have to actually be there, where your family and your responsibilities are. Try this interesting assessment: For three days, keep track of how much time you spend at home or in a direct family-related activity (like grocery shopping or going to a parent-teacher conference). Keep a second list of all the things you do in those three days that are not family oriented. You might find that some of your activities could be traded in for more family time or that some nonfamily activities get far more attention than they really need or are worth.

The Importance of Being There

All of this leads to a major bias on my part. What is my biggest worry about families? That too many parents are finding too many things to do besides being parents. In today's fast-paced, ultrabusy world, "time" for anything seems to elude most of us. The reasons that parents are not present, both physically and psychologically, are complex. The results, however, are not. They are simply that your children get less of you. They get fewer rules and guidelines. Fewer opportunities to be taught. Fewer opportunities to seek out advice and counsel. Fewer reasons to kick back and just have fun with Mom and Dad. It is clear that when parents are away from the home more than necessary, there is a significant impact on the family. If you took the last assessment and found that your "outside the family" list outnumbered your "family time" list, you may want to think about what you can do to reverse this trend. Its impact on your family should be thoroughly discussed in Family Discussion Time. Recently, a friend of mine who is a high school teacher in a neighboring state emailed me to share a new term that is floating around the high school where he teaches. It is "golden hours." Golden hours, as defined by the students, are the hours from the time when school ends (2:30 P.M.) to when the parents arrive home from work—several hours later. My friend wrote, "These kids are expert at hiding from their parents the activities they are into. Many of these activities would horrify the parents. They often occur in their empty homes."

There are parents who *must* be gone from the home more than they want to be, and there are those who *choose* to be away. No one would send children to school if no teachers were there. Most wouldn't send their children to other homes to play if no parental supervision was there. Yet, many parents leave their own children without parents *in their own homes* way too often. And this can lead to some sad outcomes. Of course, if you're reading this book, you obviously care about your children and want to be a good parent. You know that part of being a good parent is being there. Think for a minute, however, and ask yourself if you are really there enough. Naturally, you must be absent for many legitimate reasons, but do you ever justify your absence too much?

If you truly want to put your absence from the home to the ultimate test, here is what I recommend. Sit down with your children in a family meeting and talk with them about your absence. Explain what you do at work and what you do during the other times you are away. Talk it all over with them and see how they feel about it. Your children's responses will help you know if you're absent too often or if your justifications seem shaky to them.

I probably sound a bit hard-nosed on that issue. I don't apologize for it. I am a firm believer that *there are some things you can do when you are home that you cannot do if you are absent.* I implore you to sit down together and discuss your *availability* to the family. Discuss together what in your lives takes precedence over family time on a regular basis. As you discuss ways to be more available to the family, remember that there are ways to be *with* children that require your physical presence (it's hard to help a child with math homework if you can't see the assignment) as well as many ways to reach out to your children and stay in touch with their lives so they *feel* you are with them. If you can squeeze out more time to be there after school or in the evenings or mornings, your "on-site" presence will be invaluable. If it's impossible to find more time, you will need to be creative in Family Discussion time and brainstorm ways to overcome your physical absence. You might find ways you never thought of that would show your love and feelings over time and distance. Be creative. You can do it! Your children need you there.

Family Discussion Time is crucial. As parents, you must have some time each week to stop all the demands that are on your shoulders and think about your family. I hope you can find a time when you can get out your family notebook and even take ten minutes to jot down some ideas on ways to stay in touch with your children while you are away from them, or to increase the quality of your contact with them when you are home. Things you might consider are making a quick phone call from work or preparing some love notes for each one, with a stamp on it, to mail on your way to work one day. Putting a note in a lunch box helps a child—or spouse—know you are thinking of him while he is away. Just "I love you" on a piece of paper taped to a plastic sandwich bag will help. You might be surprised at the results of doing just a few extra things. You may see more cooperation or understanding from your children and spouse and thus see your burdens lightened. You can make your "little extras" as simple or elaborate as you want. What matters is that you are concerned about your absence from your children, and actions like these might help *you* and *your children* feel better. Your children notice when you intentionally work at being a parent rather than letting the days slide by without your intervention.

Many dads—and even moms these days—likely arrive home from work very tired and hardly prepared to dive into family life. To help you face these tiring and stressful moments, be creative. Listen to some peppy music to wind down on the drive home so you can greet your family with a smile and a little bit of energy. You might even want to make a deal with your kids that you get a short break, *just for yourself*, for the first 10 to 15 minutes after you arrive home. Of course, if you make this deal, you might also want to offer something in exchange, such as gathering together to read a story or play a game before dinner. At bedtime you can have a regular story time that your children can count on. I find that children get along much better if there are *traditions* or *regular events* they can count on, such as those just mentioned. Your children will do better if they have some good and happy moments that they can regularly anticipate. I often worked two or three jobs while my children were growing up. I would usually arrive home very tired. I knew I needed to spend some time with the family but was really tired. How did I do it? I would say to myself, "Remember, Jim, these are not just anyone. They are your family."

Being "Psychologically Present"

Related to the idea of being present and on the premises as much as you can is the idea that you must also be "psychologically present." That means that when you are there, you are *really* there! You must be emotionally present and available to your children.

Some parents are on the premises but always involved in something else, which makes them psychologically unavailable to their children.

A student once told me that his family would joke about their dad not being psychologically present in the family. One day someone asked if anyone had seen him. Another responded with, "I think I saw his body go by about twenty minutes ago!" Has this ever happened to you? It's fine if it happens only occasionally, but if it is a *pattern* when you are at home, it would be wise to take a look at it. When you are at home, give yourself to your children. Attend to them so they feel you are with them.

Here are three ways to do it:

1. Your children are in the living room playing a board game. You have been in the kitchen for a lengthy period of time, not really paying attention to them. You sense that you are a little disconnected at this moment. You realize it's been a few days since you've had any meaningful interaction with them. You get up, go in the living room, sit on the couch, and watch them play. You join in the conversation and smile at them as they play. It's a simple thing, but it provides an emotional connection and shows your children you are not only there for them but are also aware of them.

2. Your son is at the kitchen table doing math homework. You have been home since 6 P.M. It's now 9 P.M. You realize you've hardly talked with him in those three hours. You decide to join him at the table and get a little conversation going. "Do you need any help with that math? It's been years since I've done a math problem, but I'd love to brush up on it. Show me how to do it." Again, it's a small connection. One you probably make all the time. Next time you do it, think about the impact something so small has. It tells your child that you care about what he is doing.

3. It's Saturday, and you and your husband have spent all day cleaning out the storage room. Early in the evening, your kids

venture down to the storeroom. "Mom, Dad, we ordered a pizza. It's here. Come up and eat with us!" If you keep working, you'll be finished within an hour. You start to say that the kids can go on without you. But then you change your mind and decide to take a break and spend an hour with them.

It's Up to You

My appeal is plain and simple. *Be there for your children, physically and psychologically.* Be careful in justifying your need to be somewhere else. If you can, change your schedule and make more room for family time. If you can't change your schedule, change your thinking and find ways to be available even if you're not on site. To all parents, regardless of your parenting circumstances, I say, make yourself available all you can.

No other relationship is quite like that of a parent and child! As a parent, you can have an impact on your family that no one else can. Don't miss it.

As you do this, don't forget the one person who matters most to the success of your family: YOU! You may be reading this and feeling overwhelmed with your charge as a parent. You may be needing a break. Parents must have time off from parenting. You deserve and need regular time-outs from your daunting responsibilities in the family. Rest and relaxation for parents is absolutely essential. (For single parents, it is a greater must, since you so rarely get sufficient relief.) Please do take breaks, find time to rejuvenate and get your strength back. Take some time to yourself and then jump back into the family arena. It's far too important a role to neglect for any lengthy period of time. Parents can nurture and teach in ways that others cannot because of the natural and deep bond that is available in parent-child relationships.

Besides, why would you want to miss these experiences? Don't be fooled by people who claim to have research that indicates other adults—besides the parents—can do an effective job with children. No one wants only an "effective job" when it comes to children. We all want the *best job* done with our children. And even if someone else could do it, don't you want to be the one who is available when they have questions, fears, or successes to share? No other relationship is quite like that of a parent and child! As a parent, you can have an impact on your family that no one else can have. Don't miss it.

MOTHERS AND FATHERS

Just as mothers and fathers have different responsibilities in the family, each naturally takes on a unique and significant role. In most cases, the mother is the *heart* of the family. She has an influence on the spirit of the home and family that cannot be replicated by anyone else. There is a beautiful stability that the mother brings to the home. A mother's available and open heart makes all the difference in the family. A mom who nurtures her children with love and empathy rears children who want to be like her. As she sacrifices for her children, those same children learn principles and behaviors that will help them be more loving, kind, and moral human beings.

> *The role of mother is ultimately selfless. As your children grow, they will likely come to recognize that selfless sacrifice is the core of a mother's nature.*

The role of mother is ultimately selfless. I hope, as your children grow, that they will come to recognize selfless sacrifice as the core of a mother's nature. Mothers are so very important in the more functional family.

Because of a mother's central role in a family, there is often a misunderstanding that occurs about the father's role and responsibilities. It is the somewhat traditional view in some families that mothers should be nurturers while fathers are relieved of that aspect of parenting. I have previously described mothers as the heart of the family. I believe that. A heart, however, has two chambers, and I suggest that the other half belongs to the fathers! (Not a perfect metaphor, but I hope you get the idea.) Though mothers seem to have a special gift in the realm of nurturing, *fathers need to nurture as well.* Fathers, please make a commitment to the family to do *anything* that is needed to help make the family healthy and happy. That certainly includes nurturing, but it includes a long list of other possibilities too. Children need to see and feel their father doing whatever it takes to meet the needs of the family. A father who is unavailable to nurture his children and to participate in uplifting and strengthening his family is a huge loss to the family. The best human characteristics should be modeled by *both* the mother and the father.

Let me reiterate: The father in the more functional family needs to be willing to do whatever it takes to strengthen the family. This may include things like reading stories, helping with homework, going shopping, vacuuming, changing diapers, cooking (unless it is hazardous to the health of the children), getting up at night with a sick child, going to parent-teacher conferences, driving children to ball games, and mopping the kitchen floor, as well as the more traditional role of economically supporting the family. Come on, dads! Let's get in there and show our children that the family is so important that there is no limitation on what we are willing, even eager, to do for our families. Some fathers tell me that they are "not very good at certain family duties." My response is, "Give it a try anyway." The fact that you are willing to try carries a very powerful message to everyone in the family as they observe you trying to do your best, even when it is hard for you.

SOME ENCOURAGEMENT

I want to emphasize the importance of parents taking care of themselves and occasionally getting away from the constant demands of the family. Family life shouldn't be a prison sentence. It may sound trite, but there really are ups and downs in parenting. Take advantage of the ups. Find regular opportunity for rest and relaxation during the downs. You do not need to show such tireless devotion to your family that you end up depressed, burned out, and wanting to "run for the woods." Plan regularly for a break and some fun. Regularly. That is a must. A burned-out parent is no good. Reward yourself for all your hard work.

The more functional family needs to have a certain amount of structure and predictability to it. The individual commitment of each family member to the family is, to a certain degree, manifest by his or her willingness to identify and accept responsibility for certain key aspects of family functioning. Those commitments need to be regularly evaluated during Family Discussion Time so that family responsibilities are understood and faithfully maintained. This helps produce a sense of harmonious interaction in the family. Even if your children just fight while completing their chores and responsibilities, they are still learning how to play their own committed role in the family. They will learn most effectively by watching their parents perform their roles in a faithful and committed fashion. And while you are teaching them how to do their own jobs and responsibilities in the family, here is my (repeated) tip for success in any family activity: Children work more peacefully if root beer is waiting on the kitchen counter for "peaceful workers" to finish their responsibilities!

Using the ten-scale, rate how clearly defined and satisfactorily functioning are the roles and responsibilities in your own family._____

What are the next steps you need to take to work on roles and responsibilities in your family?

CHAPTER 12

How Do You Talk in Your Family?

While our children were growing up, I would hold a fairly regular "interview" with each of them. It was more like a chat, actually. I always started the chat with, "How are you doing?" Then, after they shared a little about what was going on in their lives, I would ask, "What would you like to talk with me about?" I always started out with those two items of conversation. After that we would talk about school, sports, friends, or other activities so they would know I was interested in what was going on in their lives.

My point in doing this was to listen. Children need parents to regularly listen to them. In such a large family it was impractical to just "hope" communication with family members would happen. There were too many people and too many details to feel secure that enough communication was happening between parents and children. I needed those interviews. I also found that informal, more casual conversations were essential. A combination of the two can really work wonders in a family and demonstrates why communication is the key to relationships.

It's Your Call

To be a success in the communications arena, you first must believe that communication begins with you. It is *your call* to really accept that how you communicate has more to do with you than with anyone else. Others influence how you communicate, but how you communicate has more to do with how you choose to respond to members of the family.

You must take responsibility for your choice of words, tone of voice, emotions, and level of sensitivity, as well as for the messages that you are communicating. Ideally, you must listen to, try to understand, and clarify what you have received from others when they talk to you. You must be caring, sensitive, honest, open, fair-minded, and unselfish. You must be just as interested in what others have to say as in what you want to say. This is a concept that every family member must ultimately come to understand. Teach it in Family Councils and Family Evenings; show even younger children that they can begin to understand and to do it. Ask them to watch you and see how you do it.

Get Feedback

Take the responsibility to find out what others in your family think. I love it when a family member asks another, "Do you feel like I understood what you were trying to say?" Many people are often unaware of how their persona affects others' ability to communicate with them. If possible, ask these questions of four or five people who know you fairly well: "How do I come across in interpersonal communication? Am I hard to listen to? Am I pushy, or not a good listener? Just what am I like when people try to talk with me? What are my positive points in communication?" You have to be able to put yourself on the line to ask such questions. They can produce some great insights for you to ponder.

A significant, if often overlooked, aspect of family communication is the emotional strength and weakness of each family member. A helpful activity would be to develop a list of your emotional strengths and weaknesses, and then get feedback on the list from others in the family. They might feel that something you consider a weakness is actually a strength. You might discover that because you are very secure in yourself, others in the family feel they can approach you with almost anything, good or bad, and you can listen to it and deal with it. You might discover that others see you as thin-skinned and overly sensitive. Family members walk around you on eggshells and are somewhat afraid to communicate anything they think you would not want to hear. Being aware of such emotional strengths and weaknesses may help you understand how you are likely to communicate in the family. When asking others for their opinions, choose family members who know you fairly well, and in whom you have a certain amount of trust. This all takes emotional openness, which is not always easy to come by.

Why is listening to others so that you can receive their feedback so important? Others hold the key to understanding how you come across to them. No parent really wants to be viewed as intimidating or unapproachable. Listening to feedback will help you know if you are communicating to your children that you are unapproachable or frightening. And, while it may be scary to elicit such feedback, if you approach the situation with humility and sincerity, you can learn much about yourself. Your view of yourself can become much more accurate and complete. A tennis player who has a weakness in her serve but doesn't know it will be appreciative of the person who points it out. That way she can overcome it and become a better player. The parent who has a difficult time communicating will benefit from feedback from family members. This feedback will help her become a better parent.

At the same time, you should be careful not to get too caught up in what others think of you. All of us care about what others think to some degree. But it's good to recognize that some people provide inaccurate feedback. It's also not wise to base decisions purely on what others will think of you. Do what you know to be right and good. You'll be able to see when there is something of benefit in the feedback you receive. When you find that, you can learn many things about yourself and undoubtedly identify an area or two where you need to do some work. For many who have tried this approach, it has become a turning point in personal communication in the family—a chance to learn about themselves, to grow, and become what they really want to be. Finally, don't assume that all your feedback will be negative! You may get a lot of positive feedback that will help you know what to keep doing.

PRACTICE INTERPERSONAL SHARING

Another extremely important aspect of family communication is being willing to participate in interpersonal sharing. Such sharing involves opening up and letting people know you more intimately and completely. It is sharing what is inside you by letting other family members know it. Some feel there is a personal risk in this. That is why it is best done in the family, where you are loved and respected. Be aware that some "sharing" can be done inappropriately and in inappropriate settings. I generally do not like public "self-disclosure programs" that people pay to participate in. Individuals can experience unnecessary feelings of being out of control in such settings. Approach them cautiously. In the love and safety of the family, however, remember that you can learn to open up and let people get to know you and your thoughts, feelings, and values. In a family that shares with each other, each person becomes a treasure. Family members want to enjoy each other and learn from each other as they share. That is the healthy objective of such sharing in the family. Communication is a central part of such interpersonal sharing. If you are going to do it, the family is the place to start.

For some, of course, sharing is tough, even in the much safer setting of the family. Be patient with each other. Do it in safe ways at first, but open up. Tell how you feel, and what you care about. Go sit by someone and talk about whatever feels most comfortable at first. Just talk. Don't be afraid to let your children know you. You might discover this is more fun than you thought. Generally, it pays off. Use a Family Evening to hold a "Getting to Know Each Other Night." On such a night, the family takes turns sharing experiences and feelings about various areas of life. Here are some discussion topics: the time you were happiest; the time you felt most afraid; your most embarrassing moment; the time you were the angriest; the time you felt best about yourself; the time you were the saddest; the time you were the most spiritual; the time you were the most depressed; the time you felt the most misunderstood; a time you learned a big lesson that changed your life in a major way; the time you felt most loved; a time when you tried to share love and how it felt; the time you felt most nervous. You could even pass out this list and let family members choose what they want to share. Then no one feels forced.

Always tell the family when you intend to do something like this so that no one feels coerced into it. Whatever you choose to talk about should be appropriate for a group meeting of whatever ages of family members are present. In a more private setting, you might share deeper feelings.

To participate in such family sharing, you need to be willing to be vulnerable. Sometimes this can be done in a larger family setting, but quite often it might be preferable to do it in a private conversation with only one child or with only your spouse. You could, for example, share with your spouse, in a private conversation, that you are feeling like a failure in your career and you don't know what to do about it. *Don't isolate yourself from the family.* Let them in on how you are doing and feeling, so that you can take advantage of the mutual support system that a family can be.

Most families can develop a sense of confidentiality, true care, and concern for each other. Don't feel like you need to maintain a certain image in the family because you don't dare let anyone know you are human or that you get discouraged or feel insecure. Families work together better when everyone realizes that fears, insecurities, and inadequacies exist in *all of us,* and we can help each other with them *if* we are open and honest in the family. It is healthy for the children to know that even parents struggle in certain situations. Children often report that they feel more understood when they know their parents struggle. A Family Evening activity that can be very bonding and unifying is discussing the topic, "My greatest fear is . . . "

I have a friend who has been suffering from depression for a number of years. We were talking about it one day, and I asked him if his family was supportive of him in his dilemma. He said, "They don't know about it." I was surprised and asked him why. He said, "I don't want them to know; I think it would affect their opinion of me." I thought that it was very sad that this man was in trouble and could not share that fact with the people who undoubtedly loved him most.

BE EMOTIONALLY OPEN

To be able to participate more fully in interpersonal sharing or to receive feedback, you need to be emotionally open. In some families emotional openness is not modeled. The children do not see it, so they don't know how to do it. Emotional openness comes when parents show children that there are a variety of legitimate emotions that can be expressed at home. In the more functional family, in fact, it is very desirable to express different emotions and feelings. Emotions tell a lot about what is going on in the family and about how we relate to each other. Often we overlook or avoid the message of emotion. But strong positive—as well as negative—emotional patterns tell us a lot about how family members are feeling and how they are getting along.

Take note that negative emotions are somewhat problematic. Negative emotions can cause damage. But you don't want to entirely avoid them because you want to teach your children how to recognize when they are feeling negative emotions and how to learn from those feelings. It's okay to be angry, depressed, or stressed out. But children—and parents—need to learn how to manage these emotions and not use them as weapons to harm others. *So, what can you learn from negative emotions?* Well, if you notice you are angry for a period of time, wouldn't it be wise to ask yourself, "Why am I feeling angry? What does my anger mean about my life or my family relationships?" Maybe, by answering those questions, you can learn some very important things that will, over time, help improve things in the family. Perhaps someone else in the family can help you understand your emotions.

If you are having frequent headaches and feeling a lot of stress, maybe you need to take a walk and ask yourself, "What are my headaches and stress telling me about my life? Maybe I need to change something." Emotions can tell you a lot about what is going on in your life, both inside and outside the family. I remember telling a couple with some marital unhappiness to go home and during Family Discussion Time simply write down the three emotions they had felt most in the last few weeks. I then asked them to share those emotions with each other and with me at their next visit.

The wife identified her three primary emotions as insecurity, distrust, and impatience (notice that all three are negative, even though I didn't ask for a list of negative emotions). The husband listed his as agitated, depressed, and content. I asked them to spend a little time just sharing with each other how those emotions came to be part of their daily lives. They told a type of "self-story" to each other, which included some significant events. The wife noticed that all her emotions were negative and were pointed toward her husband. She was surprised to learn that she had been expecting him to change and thus make her happier. She had not considered what she could do to be happier.

The husband's major surprise came from realizing that although he felt agitated and depressed at times, he was actually quite content with his own life, independent of his wife. He was agitated over their marital squabbles. He felt quite helpless about a resolution, and that's what made him depressed on occasion and unwilling to try to change.

As they opened up and shared their emotions, they created a channel of mutual understanding and began to work together to solve their problems.

Emotions can be teachers in the family, telling you a lot about what is going on in your life and family relationships. The question to ask is, "What is this emotion telling me about myself and what is going on in the family?" Please don't be afraid to talk about emotions in your family. They just might tell you some very important things.

Of course, this does not mean that you should just throw all your emotions and all your feelings at everyone in the family constantly and indiscriminately. Some degree of sensitivity and timing is necessary. Be careful and choose the right time and place to share emotions, but don't close them down and hide your emotions. If you do so, other members of your family will not really know you, how you are doing, how you feel about family relationships, and other things that are going on in your life. If your family does not know you emotionally, then they are limited in their relationships with you. Try sharing yourself emotionally in appropriate moments. You will see some good things come out of it. One warning may be needed here. If you find that attempting more emotional openness creates deep divisions and dramatic negativity, then you may want to take it very slowly or seek professional help to guide you through the process of increasing emotional openness in your family.

Those on the receiving end of another family member's attempts to communicate more openly need to show sensitivity. Even if you do not fully agree with the content of the communication, it is important to acknowledge it and be respectful of other family member's attempts to more openly communicate. Don't shut others down too quickly. Help them keep trying.

Be at Peace with Yourself

As a part of your effort toward emotional openness, you will want to seek to be more at peace with yourself. Part of being at peace with yourself means being able to merge knowledge of your positive traits with knowledge of your imperfections. No one is perfect. All of us are everyday parents living everyday lives. As you identify your imperfections and get to know and understand them, please do so with a good amount of personal tolerance and patience. As you identify those areas, you may, at first, feel discouraged. That is okay; but don't let the discouragement hang around too long. Seek to exchange discouragement for hope. Honest self-awareness is the first step in creating hope. Once you see the areas in yourself that need work, you can begin to make progress. That is a hopeful first step. Ask for help if you need it.

People in more functional families know that identifying imperfections is a step toward growth. Parents should contribute to a family atmosphere that accepts imperfections. A family that must promote a nearly flawless public image is unlikely to undergo honest self-exploration. Don't let your family fall into that trap. It's really okay for a family to be a group of people in progress. Family members should reach out to each other in hope and confidence that they can improve and grow and that it will be a mutual effort among family members.

In my professional career, I have challenged many people to acknowledge and talk about *both* their positive and negative personal characteristics. In doing so, I hoped they could realize that even negative characteristics are a legitimate part of them. Of course, negative characteristics are worth altering; but, in the meantime, members of a more functional family will

It's really okay for a family to be a group of people in progress.

recognize that everyone has areas where work needs to be done. It is healthy to have adequate respect for yourself in both your strengths and imperfections. Consider your imperfections as projects that can lead to growth. Teach that to your children. It takes openness, courage, humility, and confidence in your potential to acknowledge and work on your imperfections. Talk to any person in their later years of life, and ask about what they value most in themselves. Then ask how they got those valued characteristics. You will likely hear a story of overcoming and persistence. Had they not been, at some point in time, less developed in those areas of current strength, they could not have been afforded the opportunity to push ahead and grow.

When we acknowledge only the "good stuff" in ourselves and hide from the rest, our self-perceptions are incomplete. We know only part of ourselves. When people tell me they won't look at themselves honestly and completely and find what needs some work, I wonder what they are afraid of. Well, I know what they are afraid of! Finding damage. Being embarrassed. Sadly, they may never get to know their best selves, because their best selves are a future product—one that comes after overcoming weaknesses and accepting imperfections.

Emotional honesty is an important part of family communication. Individuals who are not aware of themselves and sufficiently at peace with what they have found tend to be more thin-skinned and self-protective and thus less open and honest with others. They take offense more easily. Those who are aware of their own personal weaknesses and are at peace with them are able to turn to others more. They tend to be less self-protective and more understanding that we all face similar personal challenges. They listen better and are less judgmental. They can better tolerate the weaknesses in others. They are happier through being more self-tolerant and self-understanding. To the degree that they feel that way, they can interact and share more openly and fairly with others. It is crucial to develop such self-tolerance, as it leads to increased acceptance toward ourselves and our limitations and imperfections. All of this helps individuals be less troubled with themselves. Their personal waters are calmer, and family members who come floating by experience less rough water!

A couple of years ago, I was asked to give a presentation at a conference on a topic that I could approach either "academically" or quite openly regarding myself. It was going to be on TV all over the United States and potentially many foreign countries. I knew I could give a satisfactory academic lecture on the subject and no one would fault me. No one would even know that the "other talk" could have been given! Guess what I did? I gave the "other talk." It was a talk in which I filleted myself in front of a very large audience. I talked about myself as a young father with a bad temper who was way too hard on his children. I exposed *Personal grievances are just extra-heavy baggage that weighs us down as we try to draw closer to others in the family.*

the weaker aspects of myself quite thoroughly. I talked about coming to the realization that I was hurting the people I loved most. Unless I faced myself and took on a major personal rehabilitation project, I predicted much unhappiness for myself and my family. I said that on TV! Afterwards, I received a ton of email from people thanking me for what I did. Many said that it gave them the courage to face themselves and quit pretending to be something they knew they were not. One of my professional colleagues, who saw a replay of the talk months later, stopped me one day and said, "How in the world did you do that?" I played dumb (comes naturally) and said, "Do what?"

"How did you lay yourself out there like that? Wasn't it embarrassing?"

I said, "I *was* kind of embarrassed." There were people in the local audience, when I gave the talk live, who had known me for years and knew nothing of what I talked about. I think many of them had a fairly high opinion of me. I had to risk losing that by giving the talk. Why do you think I did it? I did it because I was forming a club. It was the "Jim MacArthur is getting honest with himself and likes himself better that way; would you like to join me?" club. I am happy to report it has an ever-growing membership, as long as they keep replaying that talk!

As others in the family see you learning about yourself and growing, they may feel inclined to do the same. There is a spirit of personal honesty, acceptance, tolerance, understanding, and fair-mindedness that comes when family members join together in this process. We are all strong in some ways. And yet we need help in others. We can all join together in a process of growth and development. This happens best in the family. Mean-spirited criticism of each other should be avoided. Don't run faster than you have strength. Work patiently. On the ten-scale the number after 4 is 5—not 9!

SELF-PROTECTION AND PERSONAL GRIEVANCES

Within the family, those who are easily offended are usually trying to protect themselves. Quite often they do not have a very solid opinion of themselves and fear any further damage from the outside. They, therefore, move into a self-protective style of relating to others. Are you like this? If so, I challenge you to do something about how you react to others. For every ten times you start to feel offended by someone, choose to respond only to one or two, and choose those very carefully. You won't remember most of them in a week, anyway. Don't hold on to grievances. Grievances usually hurt you much more than they hurt the other person. He or she may not even know you hold the grievance. You could run around angry and hurt, and the other person could be quite unaware of it. How much sense does that make? If something needs to be addressed, take some private time with the other person and attempt to work it out. But don't hold on to it and let it eat at you. I once heard someone say, "Even if you have a genuine grievance, don't put it in a glass case and gloat over it. Believe me, you will travel with a lighter heart and a surer foot without it."

Personal grievances are just extra-heavy baggage that weighs us down as we try to draw closer to others in the family.

RELATIONSHIPS AND COMMUNICATION

In considering the fundamentals of family communication, it is very important to regularly and unilaterally nurture relationships in the family. Don't wait for someone else to do it first! Just get after it! Undoubtedly, most of your family relationships are not troubled. Any positive input you give them will likely pay off.

On the other hand, some relationships may be strained, and giving to them could be a tough challenge. So just give *something*. See what happens. As you do that, you will feel closer to others and they will likely feel closer to you. What will happen then? You may feel more inclined toward communicating. You will be less afraid of each other. When others in the family serve you, care about you, and are thoughtful and sacrificing towards you, you usually feel more drawn to them. You feel an increase of love and gratitude. Likely, you will sit down more often to talk. You may also begin to communicate more *nonverbally*, with smiles, winks, hugs, or pats on the back. Nonverbal expressions of love and positive regard help people in the family feel good. They help create a feeling of mutual trust in the family.

To be the object of someone else's undivided attention, even for a short period of time, is wonderful.

Go to others in the family and show interest in them. Listen to them. Watch them as they participate in their school and other activities. Compliment and praise them. Be courteous and say thank you to show thoughtfulness and sensitivity on your part. Help people in the family feel they are worth your time and attention. Don't be in too much of a hurry. Stop. Pay attention to them even at the sacrifice of other things you might want to do. They will notice your sacrifices and it will communicate how important they are to you. When talking, give your children your full attention. They will love it, and you will see that you have much more capacity to influence relationships in the family than you thought.

I have had so many people tell me that working at improving relationships in the family unilaterally not only improves their communication with others, but it has a noticeable positive effect on everything about them! Such a commitment changes you in many ways.

LISTENING

People like to be listened to. It helps them feel important, significant, and of value to the listener. Go to others in the family, talk, and listen. Ask how they are and show real interest. Should you expect it to be a reciprocal experience? Should you think, "I will listen and be interested in you *if* you do that for me first?" What if they don't do it for you? What if they don't listen to you? Ideally, your family members will listen to you. But in reality, your commitment to promoting well-being in your own family means being willing to work at communication with others independent of their responses.

Most of us are so busy that we often run by each other as we check off the next item on our to-do lists. Sometimes it is important to do that next item, but I encourage you to take some time each day to put down the to-do list and listen to someone. Show interest in others and their life experiences; it will help everyone feel better. Little ones need and love interest from adults, so don't forget them. Some of the people in your life who may not seem to need attention need it just as much as any other person, sometimes even more. Important people need attention too.

Listen to them as well. They are people, like you, who want to be cared about. Listen without interrupting and see if you can understand and acknowledge what they said. To be the object of someone else's undivided attention, even for a short period of time, is wonderful. How often does that happen to any of us?

Not long ago, one of my grandsons, age four, called me from Arizona. He just picked up the phone and punched the number his mother had programmed to dial our home. I answered and he began to talk. He speaks fairly clearly, but when he gets going I understand only about half of his words. I started to interrupt him and ask for his mother as the communication between us was not really clear. Then it hit me, "He needs his grandfather to listen to him." So I did not interrupt. I just listened, and whether I understood or not, I said every so often, "Really?" It worked great, and he kept right on talking!

Your commitment to promoting well-being in your own family means being willing to work at communication with others independent of their responses.

Apply what I call the *Rule of Listening.* That means you decide to listen without interrupting to let others fully express themselves. I talk, you listen. You talk, I listen. Show others that you listened and understood what they said by acknowledging the heart of what they said as evidence that you were paying attention. Whether in casual conversation or in problem solving, apply the Rule of Listening. That may mean you will have to be quiet for a while. For some that is a new experience! I actually had to tell a few of my clients to look at their watches when they started talking so they could follow a self-imposed rule of talking for no more than two minutes at a time. After two minutes, they could then say, "What do you think?" and allow the other person to express himself! That may be a shock to those who are used to talking endlessly!

Listening has something to do with how much you value others, their opinions, and their insights. Those who talk without stopping for long periods of time are focusing on themselves. I have often wondered what they would say if you called them on it! Do they truly have such a high opinion of themselves and their own opinions that they can't fit in others? Try this. After the person you are listening to is done, tell him you would like to be sure you *completely* understood him. Proceed to *summarize briefly* what you heard him say, and communicate it *to him* for his approval. He may slump to the floor in disbelief! It could be a whole new way of communicating for you! It is important to find out if the message you intended to communicate to another actually got there. It helps to ask the other person to tell you what she understood you to say. Be careful on that one. It is a little hard to maintain your composure at times when you are told you did *not* understand completely! So, be ready for that possibility. Repeat to yourself, "Be calm. Be calm!"

So, is communication in the more functional family different from communication in other families? It is. Let's look at some key aspects of family communication.

AN EVALUATION OF KEY ELEMENTS
OF FAMILY COMMUNICATION

Read each key aspect of family communication and then rate yourself and your family, using my friendly ten-scale.

1. The general atmosphere in the home encourages open communication

Is the atmosphere in your home restrictive? Repressive? Fun? Comfortable? Or does it evoke fear? How does it feel to you?

How does it feel to others? Are your children encouraged to speak up and do so often? Can everyone trust each other and the communications given?

Try evaluating these areas in your next Family Council. Give each person a piece of paper and ask him or her to describe the atmosphere in the home. Then take time to let each person share his or her opinion. It can be quite illuminating.

If you suspect that the atmosphere is troubled, then you could start out the family discussion by saying something like, "I am going to give you a sheet on which you can write a short description of the atmosphere in our home. I am asking for your honest input because I'm concerned it might not be what we want. I thought you could help by giving your opinion." That might loosen everyone up and give them permission to be honest about how it feels in the home.

The atmosphere of the home is essential to good communication because it sets the stage for so many things that go on in the family. Children need to feel free enough to express themselves, whether it be in a public family discussion or a private conversation with Mom and Dad.

As part of your discussion, consider how the general home atmosphere affects your family communication. Using the ten-scale, evaluate this statement:

The general atmosphere in the home encourages open communication._____

2. Parents are careful not to present themselves as excessively rigid thinkers

Rigid thinkers are inflexible and hung up on their own "right" opinions. Others feel put off by them. As a parent, you should avoid presenting yourself as someone who won't entertain ideas or opinions different from your own. No parent wants his children to think he doesn't—or isn't willing to—understand what they have to say.

If you have the tendency to always have to be right, try changing the way you approach things. When you know you are right and are driving on to victory, slow down, try to be patient, and think things over. Just by slowing yourself down you might realize that being right is not the most helpful thing in a given situation. Is being right more important than your relationship with a child? Is there something more important right now than winning? Many people find a way to win the arguments, but lose the relationship in return. Try to consider why you have such a need to be right. Help someone else be right for a change. She will like it as much as you do. Also, whenever you know you are right, try assuming you might not be. You will be perceived as less rigid and hung up on yourself.

Many people find a way to win the arguments, but lose the relationship in return. Try to consider why you have such a need to be right.

One way to stamp out rigid and overly dominant parental thinking is to involve others in decision making, planning, and problem solving. Don't just decide for everyone else. Use Family Councils and Family Evening. Sit down together and put before the family the issue to be discussed. Let others talk and express themselves. Wait a while before you say anything. You could discuss a family trip, a problem in the family, or a need to improve in a certain area, such as doing chores. Give each person an opportunity to express a thought or viewpoint (even the little ones, as it helps them feel important). Give everyone a chance to contribute. Put their ideas on a whiteboard. Ask for other thoughts and ideas, list some possible solutions, and take a vote.

Participation helps family members learn how to solve problems in a group, and also it helps them feel like valuable members of the overall group. They learn their ideas are legitimate and will be heard.

Show respect for your children's points of view, even if you somewhat disagree with them. Children in a family need a parent about whom they can say, "Oh, my dad, I feel safe with him. He listens to me even when I know he doesn't agree with me. He is fair with me. I don't feel like he always has his mind so made up that he won't even give me a chance to explain myself. I feel that way even though I know his values and commitments are very clear to him and to me. Because he listens to me, it makes me want to listen to him. I learn a lot from him that way, and he learns from me too." Your children want to see you as strong and confident, but also as fair-minded. That builds trust. Resist rigid, inflexible thinking on your part. Fairly consider the point of view of another, even if you disagree with it. You can be firm and clear without being rigid and inflexible.

One of the greatest abilities you can develop is the ability to see a situation through the eyes of another person in the family. Quite often in interpersonal communication, we focus on ourselves too much. While the other person is talking, we are not really listening, but are getting our own "speech" ready to be heard. That is typical, but try to avoid it and truly focus on the other person. For example, when talking with your wife or daughter, ask some questions to encourage her to explain completely what she is trying to say and help her to continue to express herself so she can fully enjoy sharing her thoughts. Think about what she might be feeling as you listen to her. By getting inside the other person's heart and mind, you will understand her better and appreciate her more. Ask yourself, "How would I feel right now if I were in her place?" As you give to her in that way, she will more likely respond similarly. This will enhance your relationship *and* foster good interpersonal communication. Using the ten-scale, evaluate this statement:

I am careful not to represent myself as a rigid thinker._____

3. *Family members take time to talk*

One of the characteristics of a more functional family is that family members actually talk and communicate. This talking and sharing can take many different forms: It can be "small talk" or more serious talk about things of personal relevance. In healthy families, parents talk because they *like* communicating with others in the family. This does not mean they have to talk all the time, although in some families they do! But they take time to talk so that they can enjoy the experience of being a family. It is sad to see a group of wonderful people, who actually are a family, become distant and lose their interest in communicating with each other.

One of the greatest abilities you can develop is the ability to see a situation through the eyes of another person in the family.

At the same time, parents should recognize that emotionally healthy people usually need some private time. Parents should not be upset if family members sometimes choose not to participate in some family activities. Children may just need some time to be by themselves. Some families suffocate the members by insisting that they be together, interacting, too much of the time. Guilt is sometimes used to force members to join in activities when they need some time alone. Try to avoid that.

Using the ten-scale, evaluate the following statements:

I take time to talk to my family._____

I recognize that my children need private time._____

4. Family communication is direct, honest, and clear

If you are *direct*, your communication goes straight from you to the person intended, rather than trickling through other people before arriving at the person you should have communicated with in the first place. If you are *honest*, you are sincere and forthright in your communication with your children. You give them what they need to know so that they can respond. You avoid emotionally dishonest communication, where you say one thing but mean another, leaving your children to figure out your real intent. If you are *clear*, after you communicate you ask the other person if he has any questions or needs any clarification from you. You say you want to be clear so that your children fully understand what you said. You want to field any questions or concerns just to be sure your message came across clearly.

By being direct, honest, and clear, you banish fear from interpersonal relationships in the family. Fear creates an environment in which self-protection is necessary. Little is left for open and honest communication. To determine how much fear exists in a family environment, the ten-scale is very helpful. That could be followed by a discussion of it in Family Discussion Time.

One of the ways you can nullify the potential presence of fear—and enhance direct, honest, and clear communication—in a family is by using softness and gentleness when you interact and communicate with your children. Both men and women can do it. Some believe softness and tenderness are female characteristics. That may be the traditional view, but men need to develop them too. Try speaking delicately. It affects how your messages are received. Reduce harshness in your tone of voice. Don't be rough. If softness and gentleness are parts of how you communicate in your family, you will likely become more approachable. Approachability is crucial in family communication. Do family members come to you easily or with apprehension? Think of other parents you know who are or are not approachable in their families. Why would that be? You could also discuss this topic in an upcoming Family Discussion Time meeting. Using the ten-scale, evaluate these statements:

I am appropriately direct._____

I am appropriately honest._____

I am clear._____

My method of communication does not evoke fear. _____

5. Beneficial outcomes are sought for both parties

After you finish communicating with a child, do you want her to feel as good about herself and what you talked about as you do? Don't enter communications to win. Pursue the communication with an entirely different objective in mind—mutual understanding and satisfaction. Enter with a commitment of mutual benefit. Until you see mutual benefit occurring, continue to try to help yourself and the other person understand each other. Ask yourself, "Does *she* feel as understood and as good as she wants to feel about this communication we are having?"

Do not enter communications to win. Pursue the communication with an entirely different objective in mind— mutual understanding and satisfaction.

Such an attitude in the midst of problem solving is a tough thing to pull off in a family because emotion can get in the way. When there is a problem with someone in the family, the natural tendency is for both parties to establish their views as the right ones in order to win the argument. If this happens with you, you may need to remind each other of your mutual purpose in trying to solve this particular problem. Say something like, "Let's not forget that what we are after here is to understand each other, so that both of us feel satisfied when we are done. I don't want to win this argument. I want both of us to be happy with the outcome of our discussion." That sets the tone for a much more understanding and amicable exchange. Now, if you do want to win much of the time, then I recommend you wrestle with your attitudes. Why do you want to win *in the family?* Winning on a soccer field is one thing, but winning in the family in the midst of interpersonal communication is quite another. To leave other family members in the loser category after talking with you is of questionable value. Using the ten-scale, evaluate this statement:

I seek mutually beneficial and satisfying outcomes in family communication._____

6. *Emotionally charged words and a negative tone are avoided*

Most interpersonal communication is nonverbal. It has less to do with *what* you say and more to do with *how* you say it. Parents should practice using mellow tones and a kind approach with the words they chose. Watch out for high peaks of emotion. Heavily emotional language is generally negative and causes the intended content of what you are saying to be missed. Ask someone to give you a "grade" on a personal characteristic like this. Tell your spouse that you are going to try some new things in how you talk to others in the family. Tell her exactly what to watch for. Then say, "You can even grade me. Give me an A, B, or C. If it's less than a C, just gently tell me that I have lots of work to do! And then tell me why. I will try to learn from what you tell me." This also creates a helpful alliance designed to promote improvements in the overall functioning of the family. I bet I know what you are thinking if you are reading this book *for* your spouse: "There is no way he will ever take that kind of feedback!" Start with yourself. If you have a spouse who is not good at taking feedback, try this approach yourself and then see if he catches on. You can't do it for him, only for yourself. You can discuss it in Family Discussion Time, though. It takes courage to face someone who typically does not take any type of feedback well. Opening yourself up to the scrutiny of others takes humility along with courage. But give it a try. Is this nonverbal aspect of family communication in good shape in your family? Using the ten-scale, evaluate this statement:

I avoid emotionally charged words and a negative tone in my own communication._____

7. Judgments are not made too quickly, and family members don't make an issue out of everything

Some people tend to form quick judgments and opinions. Try taking longer to form your opinion about a given situation before you open your mouth! Stop, be patient, slow down, and listen to others before you jump in. What you eventually say will be better thought out and hopefully more sensible if you do this. When you do speak, say less than what you normally might say. Everyone will like that. Exchange the time saved from your usual amount of talking and trade it for more listening.

Decide what is truly worth "going to the mat over" before you make an issue out of something with another family member. Ask yourself, "Should I make an issue out of what we are discussing right now, or should I just leave it alone?" Let others in the family be right some of the time. When you are coming to a point of crisis with someone in the family, see if you can stop and say, "Let's do it your way this time. Really. No judgment. No grudge. I am going to do it according to your wishes with no strings attached." You may not choose those exact words, but that is the idea. You will have a happy person on your hands, and you will probably feel better too. Using the ten-scale, evaluate these statements:

I am not quick to judge others in my family._____

I don't make an issue out of everything._____

8. Family members speak for themselves and not for others

People do not like it when you try to speak for them. Let them speak for themselves. Give "I" messages rather than "you" messages. Saying "I would like to tell you how I understand what you just said or did" is much more conducive to good communication than saying "You said or meant this or that." Most people don't like it when someone tells them how they should feel or what they intended to say.

I hear this all the time in marriage counseling. One partner will say, "You really don't care about this relationship. As a matter of fact, you don't care about anything in this family. I can tell that because you are never here and I am left with the house and kids to take care of, almost as if I were completely alone." What's wrong with this statement? It is not what she said, but how she said it that could be a problem. She was sending "you messages." Turning it around and saying something like "I feel very alone in this relationship. I feel like I am taking care of the house and the kids all by myself. It is very hard on me. I feel like you don't care much about this relationship. I would like to know how you really feel" would work much better because she would be taking ownership of her own thoughts and feelings. The second statement does not come across as an attack like the first statement did. So don't get caught up in the legitimacy of your arguments; instead, focus on how you *deliver* your words. How is this one working in your family? Using the ten-scale, evaluate this statement:

I do not speak for others in my family._____

9. *Family members talk to each other in a level way*

Do not talk *down* to others. Don't take a superior position in your communication with others in your family. Don't do this even with children. When you talk down to others, it makes them feel small, and they experience less personal value. Children are already physically smaller than you, so don't add insult to injury by talking down to them in demeaning ways. You pay way too high a price for what you get by "winning" a debate. Talk to others in a respectful manner. Be direct, honest, and clear in your communications, but not overly aggressive. Words can hurt more than we think, especially when used as weapons.

A superior approach to others has a tendency to push them aside and communicate, "I have this figured out, and I don't need your input." Some of us take a superior attitude in dealing with others due to our own sense of inadequacy. Some do not speak in a level, person-to-person way because they have a need to have more power than the other person. Some are arrogant and are caught up in themselves.

If you truly value other family members and would like to help them feel they can make a significant contribution in the family, then you must choose words and ways of talking that help them feel *included* rather than *excluded.* This is most important with smaller children. During Family Councils in the MacArthur house, we would often discuss ways of improving things in our family. In these discussions, the older children frequently offered some very mature and perceptive suggestions. (At least, they thought what they said was mature!) It would have been easy to skip over the little ones. But we tried very hard to ask them for their opinion as well, so they would feel included in our family and sense their own importance as a family member. In one discussion, we made a point to ask one of our youngest children what he thought. "And Mark, what do you think about this?" Sherri asked. Mark was our ninth child and might have been about four years old at the time. He answered, "Be good." He said that to a lot of questions. I told him, "That is a great idea, Mark. We should all be good." And, actually, Mark was exactly right!

Speaking to others in the family in a level way carries with it a very important message. It says, "You count in this family, and we will prove that to you by listening to you." Using the ten-scale, evaluate this statement:

We talk with each other in a level way._____

10. You seek the help of others in the family in order to understand your own family communication

This is one of the hardest suggestions to implement. An individual who is too focused on what he wants and how he wants things to be may have trouble communicating with other family members. He may be missing how others feel about things and how they see things in the family. The best help for this is *asking for help*. People who tend to be too self-oriented have a hard time with that request. What it takes is saying, "Look, I think I need some help. I don't know exactly how I come across in the family, but I have a hunch it is not what I want it to be. So, would you help me? I want some feedback. I want to know the mistakes I am making from your viewpoint. Would you help me by telling me the things I do in our family that are not working very well? And if there are things about me that are working for the benefit of the

family, then I want to know those too, so I can keep doing them."
That is the core idea of what you want to say. Choose your own
words, so that it sounds like you! This is a particularly helpful
thing to talk over with your partner in Family Discussion Time.
Do other family members often seek each other's help? This is a
great topic for Family Evening. Using the ten-scale, evaluate this
statement:

I seek help from others in my family._____

11. *The family has a set of rules for formal communication*

One other suggestion regarding family communication is
that you create a formal communication system in the family so
that everyone can become aware of what is going on and can
support it. Some use a family bulletin board or whiteboard. They
put the board up in an appropriate place so family members can
record calendar events and other important information. That
way everyone in the family can be aware and informed. Some use
a phone call system, in which certain people in the family are
responsible to contact and inform other family members until
everyone is "caught" in the family communication net.

Nowadays, many also use email to communicate about experiences, meetings, dinners, events, performances, fun activities,
or anything that the family needs to know about. Some use a
Website for the same purpose. Some families have a family
newsletter that they send out through mail or email each month;
each member of the family contributes an update on what is
going on in his or her life. The family newsletter often includes a
calendar of upcoming family events. This all communicates that
family matters and that you are willing to create and maintain
this type of family communication system so family members
know what is going on with everyone and can support as many

activities as is reasonable for them. Using the ten-scale, evaluate this statement:

My family has well-defined formal communication._____

CONCLUSION

Whew! You have lots of suggestions on the topic of family communication to think and talk about. Whether you do the thinking alone or with a spouse or a little of both, your underlying motivation should be that your family communicates and works together with more mutual satisfaction. You don't need to work on all of these areas at once. Pick just one to start with and go from there.

I have found that I can choose any one of the items listed above and begin to work on it. Then guess what happens? Not only do I improve in that *one area,* but I also begin to notice improvement in many other aspects of my communication! Somehow, good-heartedness and some focus in one area facilitate change in many other areas. A general spirit of caring about things that relate to your family will foster an overall improvement in you and your family.

Understanding important characteristics of family communication is vital to overall family functioning. There is a certain elusive quality to overall family communication that responds best to us simply caring about it and being interested in it. Give it some of your most committed attention.

Using the ten-scale, rate the overall strength of good communication in your family._____

What steps do you need to work onto improve communication in your family? Write them in your family notebook for later discussion in Family Discussion Time.

CHAPTER 13

Play and Have Fun Together

One of my great memories of raising our children is Tickle Time. All of my children remember it quite fondly. Tickle Time was when we would go into the family room of our home and I would chase the children around on my hands and knees until I caught one of them. I would then tickle that one until the others, seeing the plight of their brother or sister, would come and jump on me to break my grasp, freeing their sibling from the Tickle Monster. Of course, while the group of them was trying to break the captured one free, one of them would then be caught. He was then in the grasp of the greatly feared Tickle Monster. The tickling continued until that one was freed and another was caught, an endless process of saving and sacrifice. I loved it. They loved it. We would laugh and scream until we were all worn out. A great time was had by all. Tickle Time—I recommend it, as everyone has so much fun and the price is right.

Many years later, one of my daughters, having married and started a family, found a sign that she put up in her home. It read, "The Laughing Place." I liked that idea. I wondered if her attraction to the sign started back when she was a young participant in Tickle Time at our house!

Fun—It Is Essential!

Playing and having fun in your family are essential. All work and no play makes Jack and his family dull people. If you add *fun* to any other aspect of family life, your children will probably award you a gold medal. Fun can cover up a multitude of parental sins. Throw in some fun, and your children will forget the last four or five mistakes you made and even how boring you are sometimes! Fun can compensate for a lot of things.

What I have written about life in the more functional family to this point may sound awfully serious. So let me say clearly that a vital element of the functional family is that parents and children play and have fun! The functional family is not only about planning, commitment, and serious work. If fun is not a part of it, the family may break down. It's not healthy to be too serious all the time. In today's fast-paced world, you sometimes need to put up your hands and say, "Right now, we are going to laugh and play!" Slow down. Take it easy. Laugh. Play games, hold hands, take walks together, and just enjoy one another, sometimes even with little or no agenda.

Your kids will love seeing you this way. You will seem normal! And you will have more energy for family and personal pursuits. So, put smiles back on your faces. Close your planners and put away your Palm Pilots®! Don't answer the phone for a few hours. Leave your business behind for a while. Give up your drive for success long enough for some release of tension to occur. Make sure the atmosphere in your home is not too tight or heavy. Laugh at yourself publicly. Play. Goof off. Get down on the floor of your family room and chase your kids around on your hands and knees, grab and tickle them! Your blood pressure may improve and you will enjoy family life much more. Your kids will notice a difference in you. You will notice a difference too.

SPONTANEITY

One of the best ways to have fun is to be more spontaneous. Let your hair down and just hang out together with nothing planned. Families today are too overwhelmed. They have so many things they "should" and "must" do that they don't slow down and relax. I worry tremendously that with both parents working in so many cases, the parents are just too tired. They come home tired. Often they don't have the energy to even play! If you feel that way at times, it *must* become a topic for Family Discussion Time. The question to ask is: "How do we get enough energy to be able to have fun and play as a family?" Finding the answer will be good for you and for the rest of the family. A practical suggestion for having fun with family members is to see how both children and parents in your family define fun. Don't make having fun a big project, though. Occasionally you can discuss and plan for fun, such as in planning for a major family trip, but fun activities that are spontaneous and put together quickly are really exciting. They make you "drop things" and go after a fun experience quickly. You can be in the middle of a family work project and just announce, "Who is tired of this? Let's go for ice cream and finish later!" That is fun! Your children might look at you and say, "Has he flipped out?" But privately they will be giddy with excitement.

Have you ever been in the kitchen preparing dinner or mopping the floor and just stopped everything to go outside with your children and swing with them on their swing set? Have you ever been at work and had a project for which the afternoon was blocked off on your calendar, but you just packed up and left to take your teenager to hit balls at the local batting cage? Every parent's work situation is not so flexible, but check it out and see what you can do. It sends a message to your children. They will be thinking, "My parents chose between me and work, and *I won this time!*"

I have a friend who would pick up one child on Fridays and do something fun with that child. He usually did it after school or sometimes during a lunch hour at school. Sometimes it was just to go get a candy bar for a younger child. For an older child it might be to go together to buy tickets to a movie or an athletic event at the university. Sometimes he missed a week, but not very often. His kids always talked about it and thought he was a fun parent. It was not so much the length of the time but the fact that his family members saw it as something that was characteristic of his parenting.

If getting away from work is nearly impossible, then make a list of fun ideas you can do from work. Mail home a package of balloons with a note for the kids to have a water balloon fight in your name. Ever played checkers over the phone? It is fun! Or just call to set a date with the family for the very minute you get home, with fun as the only item on the agenda! It does not have to be expensive. We used to take our children to roll down the grass hills at the university when they were young. They loved it, especially if we rolled down too and then got an ice cream afterwards.

A Family Council on Fun

One great way to kick off a new round of fun activities in the family or to change the family attitude about fun is to have a

Family Council in which you try to answer this question: "What are some ways we could have more fun together?" You could get out a whiteboard or notebook and brainstorm ideas. Challenge your children to see how many ideas they can come up with in five minutes. Don't judge the ideas at first—just put them down on the board and then take a vote on which two or three you will go after first. Then get busy doing them as soon as you can! You can do simple things that don't even cost much money. For example, when our children were much younger, I would make up stories with them as the main characters. They loved it! On Family Evening you can tell the funniest, silliest, or most embarrassing thing that has ever happened to you. Children love to see their parents embarrassed. It makes you more real to them. Or you can play the stare-'til-you-laugh game. You look into each other's eyes until one of you breaks down laughing. It is a total screamer! Videotape it and watch it later. You will laugh harder watching it than you did doing it originally.

Some hold the erroneous belief that serious devotion to the most important family objectives is incompatible with fun and frolic in a family. Do you believe that? What does playing with each other communicate in the family? It says, "We like each other." And it says, "We will make time for each other." If you like each other and it is fun to be together, then you will likely get together more often. When serious times come around, you will enjoy those too.

F<small>AMILY</small> E<small>VENING</small>—P<small>ROTECT</small> I<small>T</small>

Allow me to repeat: One of my strongest recommendations for strengthening your family is to dedicate one evening per week to the family. Don't let anything get in the way on that special night. Choose Monday, Tuesday, Wednesday—it doesn't matter. But choose one! Communicate to those around you in the other parts of your life that *that* evening is *for the family*. It sends a very powerful message to your family when they see you, as parents, in the kitchen or the living room of your home ready to go for Family Evening.

You may need to notify others who could potentially interfere with *your* Family Evening and tell them "hands off of our family on this important night." It is one of the ways you have chosen to try to ensure that your family stays together and is happy. Remember, on this night you usually spend a short time learning something important, and then take all the time you like to play and have fun together. If your children are older, a smart thing to do is to attach your Family Discussion Time to the Family Evening. Do your Family Evening lesson and activity, and then excuse the children to do whatever they need to do. They could have study time to do their homework, for example. You and your spouse could then lock yourselves away somewhere and talk about your family as you regularly do in Family Discussion Time. You should be an expert on Family Discussion Time by now!

Fun People Are More Easily Approached

Think of people in your life whom you have loved and respected the most. Did they have a fun side to them that you enjoyed when it presented itself? I think we feel the greatest bond with people in our families with whom we can play and laugh. We all like people who are fun, real, imperfect, and have a goofy side that we don't fear and we don't have to measure up to. Their opinions matter more at important times. Because having fun together helps us have better relationships, we are more bonded when special moments arise in which we want to teach each other or learn from each other.

Fun people are usually more approachable. When you are in trouble you are more likely to go to members of your family with whom you have felt comfortable previously. And if you played with them previously, you have a greater chance of feeling sufficiently comfortable around them so that you can open up when opening up is important. Fun people are usually more approachable. When you are in trouble you are more likely to go to members of your family with whom you have felt comfortable previously. And if you played with them previously, you have a greater chance of feeling sufficiently comfortable around them so that you can open up when that is important. The idea of having fun in the family should not be an attitude only the parents adopt. It is one that should be promoted among all family members. It is part of a healthy family atmosphere from which everyone in the family benefits.

STRESS—SOMETHING WE ALL FACE

Families commonly experience too much stress. How do you reduce stress in your family? That is a great topic to discuss together in a Family Council or some type of family meeting, whatever you choose to call it. I love it when people are real with each other. Can you imagine in a family meeting that you might be willing to say, "I get stressed out a lot and get headaches. Anyone else ever feel that way?" How great if a teenaged child could say that and a parent could be courageous enough to say, "Yep, me too!" It is healthy to get the family together and talk about what it is like for each one to feel stress and share how he handles it.

Stress is something we all face. Yet sometimes we don't talk about these personal topics with others in the family. I wonder why. Are we trying to promote an image of being beyond such things? Again, why would we want to do that? Do you want your children to see you as someone who is above problems? If so, will they come to you when they have one? They might see you as someone who doesn't really have problems and therefore someone who knows little about them. Might they think you have become too far removed from them? Honest talking helps overcome that feeling.

You know how children recoil when you start out by saying, "Well, when I was a child, here is what I went through . . ." Avoid that intro! But do somehow let them know that you were a child or a teenager once and that you do know something about facing challenges in life. Let them know you are a real person who knows what a personal challenge is. Life has lots of challenges and stress, for both parents and children. Talking together about how to handle that stress is immensely important. Through doing so, family members may begin to see their family members as people who are a good resource when that resource is needed. Your children need to see that you are a problem solver and that problems can be faced in your family. To learn from your problems by yourself is tough. Facing your problems and learning from them in the company of family members is much easier.

Your children need to see that you are a problem solver and that problems can be faced in your family.

Stress can be so overwhelming that it can buckle the knees of a family. It can knock you down, cause depression and anxiety, and can even make you stop laughing. When you don't laugh much anymore, something is very wrong. Laughing and playing together is a great stress reducer. It not only helps us know and like each other more but it also helps us cope with the inevitably difficult parts of our lives. Taking seriously your responsibility for your family *does not* mean you have to be everything to everybody in the family all the time, or that you must ignore yourself and your own well-being. A worn-out parent won't be able to do much for the family.

Recently, someone asked me how to succeed at the more serious aspects of family life, such as sitting down together for Family Evening, where an important aspect is to help family members learn something significant. The worry expressed by this person was that it is hard to accomplish the extremely important goal of actually learning something together that the parents know will uplift the lives of family members. My feeling has always been that a key part of learning in the family is to connect it with *fun*. Remember that whenever your goal is to teach something important, keep the teaching and learning part relatively brief, approximately fifteen minutes. Tell your children that from the beginning. Tell them the challenge is to work hard together to learn something for fifteen minutes and then celebrate your joint learning with a treat and some fun! Fifteen minutes of learning followed by thirty to forty-five minutes of treats and fun is a "deal" they just can't resist! Try it. It works!

A key part of learning in the family is to connect it with fun.

Find the lighter side of family life. Laugh. Laughing contests are the best! Have a contest to see who can keep laughing the longest or who can make everyone else in the family laugh the hardest! Those are so much fun! Having fun together will help you and your children keep things in perspective. Even when you have a lot going on or have some major challenges in your midst and life seems complex, you have each other. You can put the serious parts of life aside for a bit and just have some fun together. This will help strengthen one another and develop a spirit of reassurance in your family. You are there for each other, and life won't beat you.

Rate your family on the characteristic of having fun._____

CHAPTER 14

The Extended Family– Keeping It in Good Shape

E very Sunday at 5:30 P.M. we have a family dinner at our home. The whole extended family is invited. It takes a lot of work and preparation to feed fifteen to twenty-five people. After dinner, we hang out and talk and play with the grandchildren. We have done this for about twenty years now. Every once in a while we mention that maybe we should not continue it and everyone could just spend Sunday afternoon at their own homes having their own dinner. We always get voted down. I guess a free meal is too much to give up! Actually, as good as Sherri's cooking is, the extended family relationships and the chitchatting is what keeps the event going.

It is a time when our grandchildren can get together and play with each other. Once a month we expand the dinner into an Extended Family Evening when we spend some time as adults learning about something that is mutually beneficial. It is presented by one of the adults or couples. It is kind of like a mini family reunion the last Sunday of each month! It is great to keep in touch with the broader family—no matter how you do it. It does not need to be every week, but some type of regular contact with each other is a worthwhile thing to promote. It helps keep the "feeling" of the extended family alive.

So far, I've focused mostly on how to create and maintain a healthy *individual* family. Each of your children will grow up and probably get married, have children, and likely become part of their own individual family. As they become part of their own families you will soon have a group of families, or in other words a larger extended family.

As individual families become an extended family, interpersonal relationships become more complex. It requires more of individuals to work at having healthy and happy relationships with that larger group of people. Some people come into the family by marriage, and they bring with them their own family backgrounds. Some will come with very healthy backgrounds, and others will have experienced various amounts of trouble and difficulty in their families of origin. They may not have learned in their own family how to have completely healthy and happy family relationships. Some will come from quite healthy family backgrounds, but will have different traditions and ideas about how things should be done. So, as the extended family group expands, you will find that its nature usually becomes more complex and requires more patience and understanding on the part of all involved.

WHAT IS THE VALUE OF THE EXTENDED FAMILY?

We live in a day when so many things are temporary. Things that used to last don't last as long anymore. Things that used to endure are now easily replaced. We used to be able to buy soda pop in glass bottles that would be reused. Now we buy it in cans that are thrown away or crunched into masses of recyclable material. We really don't expect to see *that* can again. When you meet someone who has been married for forty years, you are a bit surprised because you don't expect marriage to last that long in most cases. What lasts? Not many things do anymore. So, it is nice to be a part of something that endures and is ongoing—the extended family.

As the extended family group expands, you will find that its nature usually becomes more complex and requires more patience on the part of all involved.

Through the extended family, your family—really, your life's work—continues. That should give you a feeling of security and confidence in life. The members of your extended family can have meaningful and inspiring relationships. A group of families that can work together to help everyone feel significant, important, worthwhile, and valuable is an example of the great and marvelous interaction possible among human beings, all of whom are—to a certain degree—different. I believe you can talk about this interaction together in an extended Family Evening and agree that this support is one of the reasons why you join together to enjoy one another.

An extended Family Evening is just like your individual smaller Family Evenings when you get your family together for some learning, activity, and goodies, except that this is a group of families. This would be grandparents, parents and their children, and all other family members. Everyone is included.

Earlier I described the extended family as *inspiring.* That means there is something that uplifts and elevates you by being a part of this extended family relationship. Sometimes it is one or more of the individuals in the extended family that inspire you. If that occurs within your extended family, I hope that you might find a way to communicate to that person how he or she affects you. So often we think or feel those things and never say them. They don't have to be said every time you meet, but sometimes it is a wonderful gift and an uplifting experience to communicate them. A note in the mail, a phone call, or taking someone aside to tell him or her how you feel can mean a great deal to those who receive such messages.

Inspiring also means that your involvement in the extended family encourages you to live a better life. You may get a chance to observe other parents and how they relate to one another in their individual family. You may get to witness kindness, empathy, thoughtfulness, patience, endurance (especially in the parents of teenagers), goodness, courtesy, sacrifice, and so many other great qualities in the people you get to be around in the extended family. The other night I was at the home of one of my married sons, and one of his children was fussy and hard to deal with for a period of time. I watched my son deal with him firmly, but with wonderful patience. As I was driving home, I said to Sherri, "I wish I could have done it more like that when I was his age." My son was a good example to me.

Sometimes you will also witness negative examples that help you see another side of things. But even a negative example can be inspiring if it helps you commit to do better in your own life. When you see a negative example, don't just be publicly or privately critical. Use it as a way to convince yourself that *you* ought to seek a different personal path. "Keep your comments to yourself" is usually a good rule of thumb to follow in the extended family!

IT IS IMPORTANT FOR THE EXTENDED FAMILY TO MEET

I encourage you to have an extended Family Council in which the whole extended family gets together to discuss how the extended family can participate together regularly and actively. At least you can get those who live near each other together. A long-distance Family Council can also happen by way of conference phone calls, email, or letters. You can then discuss how to maintain your extended family relationship, rather than how to actually meet. An extended family is just an extended group if they don't actively relate to one another as a family. If you are able to meet, the frequency of the meeting can be whatever you choose it to be. Be flexible. Allow all the individual families who make up the larger extended family to choose how they will participate in the extended family. There should be no forcing. Every individual family has its own needs and reasons for greater or lesser participation in the extended family. But at some level, to really be an extended *family*, there needs to be some regular interaction.

An extended family is just an extended group if they don't actively relate to one another as a family.

This interaction can come in the form of family reunions, joining together for birthdays, holiday gatherings, extended Family Evenings once a month (or less frequently, if that is the decision of the extended family), or any other designated meeting time. Having a segment of a get-together for the adult members and another for the children is also a good idea. The needs of adults and children are different. Make sure there is plenty of fun and food. Then extended family members will want to come back!

When family members feel they are each an important part of the larger family, they will be drawn to whatever form of participation in it they can do. However, each individual family needs to have its own identity and its own way of doing things. The extended family should never interfere with any of that. The extended family needs to be very respectful of how individual families choose to do things and what they want to be like as families. Certainly, in discussions and communications within the extended family, all should be invited to freely share thoughts, ideas, and impressions of effective ways to do various things and what they have tried out. But this is usually done without the intention of obtaining universal agreement. The sharing that can go on in such discussions is meant to be just that: sharing.

On a practical basis, the extended family can be a reservoir of great help to all the extended family members. Now that we live in a day of almost universal email, it is wonderful to communicate broadly with family members on almost any topic. You can share impressions on topics of common interest or also seek advice and help. Over the last year, some of our adult children have been communicating their thoughts with each other on some current political topics. Some have shared ideas on things like potty training children and child discipline. All you have to do is form an email group of extended family members and then send off a quick notice to the group on a question or issue. Suddenly, where you live will no longer be an issue. You can help each other over the miles quite easily.

Some of you may have large extended families on both sides of the family. Perhaps both extended families are very involved and have lots of get-togethers and activities. That makes it more difficult to participate in everything that is going on. Please consider this with a great deal of patience. My recommendation is that once your children marry, they must have complete autonomy to make their own decisions about when and how much they participate in various extended family events. Don't put guilt on them! Some married adult children feel trapped by heavy expectations on both sides of the family. They don't know how to please everyone. Try to make it easier for them by calming your own expectations. Some of them will be dealing with very complex families and expectations. Cut them some slack and let them work it out as best they can. Just be glad when they can come and join you.

I would also encourage you, as an individual, to give some thought to what you can personally contribute to the extended family. Maybe just showing up is good enough. Just to make the sacrifice to be there will certainly strengthen the overall fiber of the extended family. That would be especially true if you are usually one who does not show up! Maybe there are petty issues that you will need to reconsider and put aside so that you can be a contributing part of the overall family. Maybe there is one relationship you will need to work on so that it does not prevent you from attending family events. If so, I encourage you to do it. Rectify it and don't let it keep you from being part of the extended family. To participate in the extended family usually requires sacrifices on everyone's part. There are times when it is not convenient to attend or participate, but you do it as a demonstration of support for the extended family. There are times when you are tired and not completely interested in the family activity or get-together, but you join in anyhow. This may not always be possible, but making sacrifices to be a part of the extended family shows commitment to the extended family.

Making sacrifices to be a part of the extended family shows commitment to the extended family.

KEEP IN MIND SPECIAL NEEDS AND CIRCUMSTANCES

Members of the extended family may have special circumstances that should be recognized. Some may be single, others married with no children, and still others married with children. Some may have older children, and some have younger ones.

Although it is often a complex issue to pay sufficient attention to all the needs in a growing extended family, it is important to remember that various family members have different needs that should be considered as much as possible. They will also likely make uniquely valuable and important contributions that should not be overlooked.

Older Family Members

There are some in every family who are getting older. You may have grandparents, as well as great-grandparents, to consider within the far-reaching bonds of the extended family. Keep an eye on the elderly members of the family. Don't let them be forgotten or excluded. It may take special sacrifices to go and pick them up and help them feel wanted and loved. Most of the time, when older family members feel unwanted and ignored, it is unintended by the rest of the family. It is just a matter of not making their welfare a high enough priority among all the things you need to pay attention to when you get together.

Give elderly members of the family opportunities at extended family get-togethers to share their wisdom and experience. You can gain a lot from them if you take the time.

Teach younger children to be respectful of the older members of the family and to visit with them and learn from them. Talk about them with reverence and honor within the family. They may have their own idiosyncrasies, but you also have yours! Tolerance for each other's weaknesses and quirks is a topic that does not get enough attention. Give elderly members of the family opportunities at get-togethers to share their wisdom and experience. You can gain a lot from them if you take the time. They have probably learned some very valuable things during their sojourn through life. Listen to them. Have some private conversations with them. Someday you won't have their voices to listen to anymore. Taping or videotaping them is a great idea for sharing with their future posterity. It is very important to help them feel important and valuable.

The older generation represents the continuity and permanence of the family. That is a great gift they can offer.

Depending on their age, elderly family members can make their own conscious contribution if they understand the role they can play. That role can be vital in the extended family. In many ways, grandparents and others in their age group have an opportunity to be examples and role models to others in the family. If grandparents understand that a big part of what they do in the family is to be an example, it might help them to see how important they can be to the rest of the family. In a certain way, it is up to them to fulfill this much-needed family role. Grandparents and older family members are major evidence that the family and family values can continue on. They are living examples of important family values; if they do nothing else but represent those values, they are doing a great service to the extended family.

The family that they started those many years ago was not temporary. I hope it has grown and been strengthened. It is continuing on; their children and grandchildren are evidence of this. Some of the older generation feel they have little to contribute as they get older. Perhaps they can't do some of the things they used to do. But they can *be* the things they used to be. They can represent the continuity and permanence of the family. That is a great gift they can offer to their extended and growing family. Help them understand that.

Grandparents can also be a great source of understanding and perspective. They can help us remember what really matters. They can talk with us and help us see, from their many years of living, the truly important things in life. Family is one of those important things. That is why they are willing to come and join with you, even though it may be hard for them to walk or even talk and interact. They are a testimony of how great it is to just be there with the family.

As I have watched grandparents, I find that one of the wonderful things they can offer to the family is a good listening ear. Often in the family, everyone is busy. We are running to and fro, and we rarely stop and give others in the family one of the greatest of all gifts: listening to them. Grandparents are great at that. They listen to the rest of us! They are doing a great thing for the family; their listening makes others feel significant and loved. We should take time to listen to them, too. Undoubtedly, the principal offering of grandparents is love. They don't have to discipline us anymore! So, they are free to just give lots of love to everyone. What a great job to have in the extended family!

The wonderful thing about the extended family is that it exists. It can be real. It started as just two people. Over time they had children. Their children grew up and married and had children of their own. Now that larger group comes together as an extended family and it continues on. The existence of the extended family shows that the family can continue over a significant, potentially endless period of time. Meaningful relationships wrapped in the bonds of family love are priceless.

Do a ten-scale evaluation on the strength of your extended family._____

CHAPTER 15

My Feelings about the Family

Studying and helping families has been a passion of mine for many years. Families are under great pressure in our society, and healthy families are tremendously hard to develop. In some sectors, respect for families is diminishing. That is a societal tragedy! I've discussed a number of concepts and practices that can help families develop and become more functional. My sincere desire is to help *your* family. I've also had a more personal goal, which is to continue to help my own family. I hope that your family and mine will be better if we do the things I've outlined in this book.

In this book you have read about the things I consider most important in building a healthier family. And *building* is a key concept. More functional families are built; they are created. Remember that as you work to make your good family better. And then just keep working toward that end because you deeply care about your family. Parents obviously play the key role in a family. As parents, it is what you offer your children, what you do for them, that is important in creating and guiding the family. Parenting is about *inviting* your children to be family apprentices so they will one day learn how to run their own families. We all want healthy families to continue on, generation after generation. Show your children how to do it.

Remember that *it does not all happen at once.* It is an unfolding and developing process. The process undoubtedly will include pain and disappointment in some of the developing moments of family growth. The family must be guided intentionally by the parents, with the utmost dedication and commitment on their part. Your children may learn how to guide their own families by watching you guide yours.

OUR PASSIVITY—FAMILIES GETTING UPSTAGED

Many in society today are too passive about the family. I believe that most people care about their families, but have allowed too many other things to upstage them: work, recreation, and personal needs. The family must come first. Plain and simple. That's it. It's the reason I've zealously promoted a regularly held Family Discussion Time over and over. Parents need to set a time to think about their children and plan for *The family must come first.* whatever the family needs. I honestly believe that if every parent would set aside half an hour each week and focus on what he or she could do to strengthen his or her family in the areas covered in this book, as well as others you can come up with yourselves, it would make major a difference in the quality of family life in this country. If you don't know where to start as you begin Family

Discussion Time, try discussing the answer to this question: "Considering the experiences I have had as a parent to date, what are the things that seem most important to pursue now in my family?" That question will help you make a list of topics that you can begin to work on as you hold your weekly Family Discussion Time.

A Deeply Personal Journey

I believe it takes a lot of caring to create the spirit—or atmosphere—that is present in the homes of more functional families. It requires that parents sacrifice and humble themselves so they can be open to learning about themselves as parents and how they affect their families. It is a deeply personal journey in which parents must vigorously strengthen themselves, challenge themselves, and seek to move to a higher level of parental leadership. Parents must set an example of personal integrity in everything they do. Their stated values and commitments must be demonstrated in the family by clear and consistent behavior for the sake of their families. They must know, within themselves, what they care about and are dedicated to. They must demonstrate those things to their children by how they treat them and how they live each day.

Parents must set an example of personal integrity in everything they do.

With that clear admonition to take it all very seriously, I also ask you not to be too hard on yourselves. You have a big job to do as a parent in the family. It is one for which each of us is quite unprepared as we embark on the journey, even if we had a healthy family upbringing. We were not the parents then, but we are now! Be patient with yourselves in all this hard work, but do take it seriously. I don't believe there is anything you will do in life of greater consequence than what you do in your home and family. I hope it is something you actually want to do. It doesn't work very well as a duty. If it feels like an obligation to you, then you will lack something important when sacrifice is needed. It needs to go a step beyond duty or obligation. You must get a vision of the family and love to work at it and in it, even with its tough moments and challenges. Gratefully offer yourself in service to those you love most—the members of your family.

Take time to regularly ponder about your family members, and then consciously work for them. It will bring you great inner peace and happiness to be able to look back one day and consider all you have offered and done in your family. In the end, that final moment of satisfaction will have been earned. There are definitely times of frustration and despair as you travel the family road. I have felt some of that myself, but I can honestly say, after thirty-five years of such travel, that I have learned a lot. I believe it has made me a better person. I am glad I did it. I would do it over again, even knowing how hard it can sometimes be. I have learned something about love by being a husband and father that I never understood before I had a family.

A family is a unit, but remember that if a family is healthy and adequately functional, then individuals should exist within the family. Everyone does not have to be exactly the same. Family members undoubtedly will hold some values and beliefs in common. Those are what I have called core family values. But each family member remains an individual and has wonderful personal uniqueness. One of the great strengths of many nations is the diversity of their citizenry. One of the potential strengths of churches or humanitarian groups is the diversity of their members. And one of the great strengths of a family is the diversity in its members.

The Real Battle

I have written a lot about outcomes and why it is more important that you offer your best rather than seek to control the outcome. Having said this, I would like to see one outcome for *all* my children. That outcome is success in the daily battle between selfishness and selflessness. Each of us fights this daily battle between being a giver and a taker. And this is our ultimate challenge as parents, to help our children choose between selfishness and selflessness. The responsibility of parents is to demonstrate to their children, regardless of age, that they, too, are making that very choice time after time, day after day. The world our children live in invites them to be self-preoccupied and excessively pleasure seeking.

> *The best place to fight the battle between selfishness and selflessness is at home in the family.*

I believe the best place to fight the battle between selfishness and selflessness is at home in the family. I care deeply about my children growing up to be more and more selfless over the terms of their lives. I hope they will find ways to be givers and contributors in life, rather than falling into the common human trap of being thoughtlessly selfish. If you want to work for something that can last—work for your family.

One of the great challenges of a family as it "grows up" and the children get older is to help them feel continually connected to their family of origin while feeling completely free to create their own new families into which their own children will be born. In that way, the process of family evolution starts over again. It is exciting to watch and experience. Children must feel encouraged to leave the nest, to go and build their own nest, and yet want to come back and enjoy the nest they came from.

Everyone does family life just a little differently. That is good.

We do it with our own personalities, values, and capabilities. I hope that this book has inspired you to consider the ideas I have offered. But mostly, I hope that it has helped you to be more thoughtful when it comes to your family. I hope it has convinced you that you need to take regular time to think about your family and how things are going in it. If it has done that, then it has done its job. Don't use this book as the final authority. But do use it to challenge your thinking and the assumptions upon which your family operates every day. Let it help you think deeply about your family and how you want it to be. I believe each of us must make a moral commitment to the family and then be true to it.

> *The family is the best organization for building healthy people and for ultimately finding joy and happiness in life.*

This book has been written with sincere and serious points of emphasis, based on my own view of what is important to address in the family. It is not given as a rigidly held viewpoint on the subject. It is one person's thoughts on the family, born of much personal and professional experience. I hope it has convinced you to pay more attention to your family and to care deeply about the family experience. I hope it is a strong voice that reaches into your heart and helps you draw the conclusion that your dedication to your family is your highest priority and privilege.

I have spent many, many years observing families. I hope what I have offered you will help you with yours. Work at it patiently but with intent. Be fair with yourself as you try to guide your family. It is hard work at times. It has been a challenge to me. My best and worst moments have come from trying to guide my family. I have given it what I knew how to give at the time. I kept trying to learn about families and never lost my hope and faith in the concept of family. I hope you will do the same. I truly believe the family is the best organization for building healthy people and for ultimately finding joy and happiness in life. God bless all of us in doing the greatest work there is to do: family work.

Index

Self-confidence, 69, 90; lack of, 52; development of, 92
Self-disclosure, 55, 213
Self-esteem, 12, 48, 116; low, 58; and children, 76–77, 92, 122; parents and, 84; threats to, 125
Self-evaluation, 29, 158, 167–68; parental, 30–39, 182; ten-scale, 106
Self-image, 6, 58, 105, 220
Selfishness: assessment of, 34; putting aside, 154; and selflessness, 263
Selflessness, 19–20, 66–67; and selfishness, 263
Self-love, 53
Self-pity, 56
Self-protection, 222, 231
Self-respect, 12–13; developing, 76
Sensitivity: assessment of, 33; communication and, 218
Service: families and, 10, 66, 68, 109; in the home, 111, 165
Sex, and intimacy, 55
Sharing: interpersonal, 213–15; emotions, 218; talking and, 230
Shyness, 38
Significance, need to feel, 119, 130
Sincerity, 145, 212
Single parents, 18–19, 115, 199
Society, family as foundation of, 11
Softness, using, and gentleness, 231
Soil, healthy emotional, 122
Solutions, generating possible, 74
Spirit: love and the human, 52; of a home, 164, 261
Spirituality, 36
Spontaneity, 242–43
Spouse, control of, 46–47
Strength, emotional, 212
Stress, 34, 216; expectations and, 85–86; reducing, 246–47
Structure, predictability and, 208
Strong-willed, 38, 39
Study: time, 181; developing, habits, 189
Success: families and, 13, 48–49, 81, 205; parents and, of children, 84, 88–89; experiences, 90; in family activities, 208

Supervision, parental, 201
Support, signs of, 98; for extended family, 255
Survey, family, 7–8
Symptoms, 51

Talking, sharing and, 230
Teachers, emotions as, 217
Teaching, 187–89: families and, 12; the important things, 174; direct and indirect, 179–80; fun and, 182; responsibility for, 185; expectations, 185–86; importance of, 186–87; and time, 189; moments, 189, 192–93; voice, 190; parental, formula, 192–93
Teasing, 105, 106
Ten-scale, 21, 27–29, 99; and blackboards, 114; and relationships, 146
Tension, release of, 242
Thinkers, parents as rigid, 227–28
Thoughtfulness, 124; assessment of, 33
Time, 127–29; giving children, 124, 144; in family-related activities, 200–201; need for private, 230; Tickle, 240
Time-outs, parents and, 205
Togetherness, 190
Tolerance: families and, 11–12, 222; personal, 218–19
Touchpoints, 143
Touch, staying in, 202–3
Traditions, family, 113–14, 203
Trouble, unpredictability of, 47
Trust: intimacy and, 55–56; insufficient, 86–87; and goals, 89

Ultraresponsibility, 54
Uncertainty, facing, 12
Understanding, 44, 222; mutual, and satisfaction, 232–33
Unforgiving, assessment of, nature, 39
Utah State Prison, 3, 150

Valuable, need to feel, 119
Value, 121; less functional families